MW01180999

Late Sophocles

for David

Thanks for your encouragement and support.

Love, Tom

3/16/15

Late Sophocles

THE HERO'S EVOLUTION IN *ELECTRA*, *PHILOCTETES*, AND *OEDIPUS AT COLONUS*

Thomas Van Nortwick

UNIVERSITY OF MICHIGAN PRESS

ANN ARBOR

Published in the United States of America by the
University of Michigan Press
Manufactured in the United States of America
♾ Printed on acid-free paper

2018   2017   2016   2015   4   3   2   1

A CIP catalog record for this book is available from the British Library.

Library of Congress Cataloging-in-Publication Data

Van Nortwick, Thomas, 1946– .
    Late Sophocles : the hero's evolution in Electra, Philoctetes, and Oedipus at Colonus / Thomas Van Nortwick.
        pages   cm
    Includes bibliographical references and index.
    ISBN 978-0-472-11956-1 (hardcover : alk. paper) — ISBN 978-0-472-12108-3 (ebook)
    1. Sophocles—Criticism and interpretation.   2. Sophocles. Electra.   3. Sophocles. Oedipus at Colonus.   4. Sophocles. Philoctetes. I. Title.
PA4417.V36 2015
882'.01—dc23

2014049364

For Nathan Greenberg
colleague, mentor, and friend

Preface

Oh children, follow me. I am your new leader,
as once you were for me.
    (Sophocles, *Oedipus at Colonus* 1542–43[1])

Sophocles's *Oedipus at Colonus* ends with his most famous character walking serenely through the central doors of the stage building (*skēnē*) in the Theater of Dionysus and into the grove of the Eumenides. For a blind old man, enfeebled by age, to make this journey is miraculous enough; that he is the play's hero is stranger still—no sign here of the familiar willful figure, defining him- or herself through defiance of higher forces in the universe. Rather, Oedipus reaches in this final exit the goal he announces at the beginning of the play: to achieve a "glorious consummation" at the end of his long and tumultuous life by obeying the will of the gods. His last walk, a riveting moment in Western theater, marks the end of Sophocles's long and fruitful career as a playwright. In the old Oedipus, he completes a reimagining of the tragic hero that stretches across his last three extant plays, beginning with Electra, continuing with Philoctetes, and ending on the last day of Oedipus's life. That evolution will be the focus of this book.

All three characters are, as we will see, strikingly original. But their enduring fascination, for scholars, for directors, for playgoers and readers of the plays, is not mysterious. In their words and actions, we encounter large questions about human life. How do we balance the demands of our often imperious individual will with the need for community? Can the egregious powers of one person be harnessed consistently for the greater good? What is the place of human life within the larger cosmos? And most insistently, what does it mean to be human, to be a creature who knows that s/he must die? As vehicles for exploring such questions, Electra, Philoctetes, and the aged Oedipus take their place beside many other examples of the tragic hero, not confined to or originating in Greek drama or even Greek epic. Such figures can be found at least as far back as *The Epic of Gilgamesh*.[2] But the rise of tragic drama alongside Athenian democracy and the centrality of the art form in Athenian public and intellectual life give the traditional heroic stories a unique and powerful resonance when they appear in the Theater of Dionysus. One of the goals of this book will be to show how the hero in Sophocles's last three plays evolves to reflect contemporary issues in late fifth-century BCE Athens.

Though there are marked differences between the last three heroes, we can see certain common patterns in their relations with other characters and their roles in the articulation of the plot of each play. Each occupies a liminal position in relationship to the central myth that drives the plot; none is typically empowered to impose his or her will on others. Ragged and disreputable, deceived and manipulated by others who would use them for their own purposes, they seem unlikely candidates for the role of Sophoclean tragic hero. In the last decade of his life, the playwright appears to have set himself the challenge of writing plays that feature the eventual triumph of a disempowered protagonist rather than the ruin of someone who is viewed with envy by others. The nature of that triumph in each case is the key to understanding Sophocles's purposes in his last decade as an artist. As we watch these unlikely heroes stubbornly resisting what the received stories require of them, our perception of traditional assumptions about behavior and motive carried in the structure of the myths is continually challenged: Can the Electra we see onstage really be healed by the deaths of Clytemnestra and Aegisthus? If Philoctetes is the chosen instrument for divine will in the fall of Troy, why is he discarded for ten years on a deserted island? And why is he chosen in any event? How can such a thoroughly reviled figure as Oedipus become the conduit for the working out of divine will?

When I began teaching Greek tragedy forty years ago, I had no direct experience with the problems faced by directors and actors who were seeking to bring the ancient dramas to life onstage. I presented the texts in the same way I did Homeric epic, as stories founded on ancient myths. Trying to explain the intellectual richness and complexity of the plays in this way was certainly challenging enough for a rookie teacher. And I was not out of step with my fellow Classicists.

Sustained attention to issues of performance has come relatively late to Classical scholarship, beginning with the pioneering work of Oliver Taplin in the 1970s.[3] Since then, a steady stream of important work on staging and performance has opened up new avenues of thought in the study of Greek drama.[4] The opportunity to work on several productions by the Great Lakes Theater Company in the 1990s added immensely to my own appreciation of these issues.

I also had much to learn about the chorus in Greek drama. The complexity of metrical structures in choral songs was (and is) daunting. Again, I have benefited from the excellent scholarship of others.[5] Likewise, creative analysis by Classicists of the choruses as "music" has enriched my own understanding of the full impact of the dramas onstage.[6] Sophocles extended the dramatic expressiveness of his choruses in his last three plays, making their songs an even more integral part of the characterization of his heroes. In place of traditional stanzaic forms, sung exclusively by the chorus, we begin to see actors sharing their entrance song with the chorus, weaving their thoughts and emotions into the complex metrical structures. The characterization of Electra, for example, is articulated in part by her lyrical exchanges with the chorus (*El.* 121–212); when Antigone leaves the stage to perform purification rites on behalf of her aged father in *Oedipus at Colonus*, past practice by Sophocles might lead us to expect a self-contained choral song, a reflective pause while action occurs offstage; we get instead an intense lyrical exchange between Oedipus and the chorus of citizens, raising, not lowering, the temperature onstage (*OC* 510–50).

It will be evident to readers that my discussion of the last three plays owes much to these new approaches. But the primary focus of what follows is Sophocles's vision of the tragic hero. There has been no shortage, of course, of excellent scholarship on this topic. Reinhardt, Whitman, Knox, Segal, and many others have all written brilliantly on the nature of Sophocles's heroes.[7] My debt to them will be obvious, and I have tried to acknowledge their ideas in the discussion that follows.

I hope my ideas are of interest to Classical scholars, but I also want to make my arguments accessible to nonspecialists. With these aims in mind, I have on the one hand retold more of the stories than experts require and I have translated all the Greek texts into English. At the same time, readers will notice that I often insert transliterated Greek words or phrases parenthetically in my translations and analysis. My purpose in this practice is to allow those who know ancient Greek to follow my thinking more closely. I regret that Seth Schein's commentary on *Philoctetes* reached me too late to be included in this book.

Acknowledgments

I began thinking about some of the ideas in this book twenty years ago, when I was asked by the Great Lakes Theater Festival in Cleveland to participate in an educational outreach program for their 1995 production of Euripides's *Bacchae*. That project put me in touch with Bill Rudman, then the educational coordinator for GLTF, and Gerald Freedman, the director of the production. I owe them both a great debt of gratitude, for allowing me to see how a professional theater company approaches the task of bringing a work of Classical drama to the stage. The time I spent talking to each man about this process sparked an interest in issues of performance that has informed my teaching and writing about Greek drama ever since.

Virtually all of my published work on Classical literature has had its origins in the classes I have taught at Oberlin College over the past forty years. I wish I could list all of the names of the wonderful students who have shared this journey with me. If you happen to read these words, you know who you are and how much I owe you. Working at Oberlin has brought me into the company of great teachers and scholars, on whose time and wisdom I have presumed in many hours of conversation. I owe special thanks to my colleagues in Classics, Nathan Greenberg, James Helm, Kirk Ormand, Benjamin Lee, Andrew Wilburn, and Christopher Trinacty. Everyone should be so lucky to work with people like these. Lewis Nielson and David Young, colleagues and treasured friends, have read and discussed drafts of this book and given me valuable feedback.

Working with the editorial staff at the University of Michigan has once again been a pleasure. Ellen Bauerle's editorial expertise and good judgment have been immensely helpful and I am very grateful to her. The three anonymous referees for the Press made helpful suggestions that have improved the book in many ways. I thank them for their careful attention.

Finally, I want thank two people whose wisdom and generosity have influenced me enormously, as a teacher and as a human being. My wife, Mary Kirtz Van Nortwick, has been an inspiration to me in countless ways. Her intelligence and loving companionship over the past thirty years have been a gift beyond measure. Nathan Greenberg has been my colleague, mentor, and friend for forty years. Most of what I know about teaching and much of what I know about being a man have come from watching and listening to him. This book is dedicated to him with my profound gratitude and affection.

Contents

CHAPTER 1 Introduction: The Artist in Old Age   1

CHAPTER 2 *Electra*: Glory Bathed in Tears   7

CHAPTER 3 *Philoctetes*: The Creature in the Cave   43

CHAPTER 4 *Oedipus at Colonus*: Spiritual Geography   81

CHAPTER 5 Late Sophocles   115

Notes   125

References   139

Index   145

Introduction

The Artist in Old Age

Yet come, Goddesses, grant my life a final boundary,
as Apollo has foretold, some great consummation . . .

(*Oedipus at Colonus* 101–3)

Sophocles died at the age of ninety in 406 BCE, with *Oedipus at Colonus* still to be produced five years later. *Philoctetes* appeared in 409, and most scholars would date *Electra* somewhere between 420 and 410, with the later date predominating.[1] To have created three such rich and powerful works at any stage of life is remarkable; to do so in one's ninth decade, at the end of a career spanning over sixty years, is astonishing. And though *Oedipus at Colonus* is certainly valedictory in several senses, none of the last three plays shows any signs of failing powers. If anything, Sophocles's mastery of verse-making, plotting, and scene construction increases in these final works.[2] We sometimes associate an artist's late works with a certain autumnal quality, a mellowing detachment from the passions that drive us in youth, but the emotional pitch and dramatic tension in these plays remain high. Coming to the end of his life, Sophocles and his characters engage the trials and mysteries of human existence with an undiminished energy. The last three plays, in fact, show the playwright developing his vision of the tragic hero, changing how these figures fit into and help to articulate the dramatic dynamic of the plays. This new paradigm, in turn, allows him to suggest new ways of seeing and understanding the knotty problems about human experience that his work always addresses.

We find Sophocles exploring new territory in his last three plays, but he has packed a bag full of earlier work. Figures and themes from his earlier plays pass over the stage, now reworked and developed in new ways. Alongside them are the great Homeric characters, always present in Sophocles's dramas, providing threads of continuity with the heroic past.[3] Electra, as the woman who waits for the hero to return home, carries a penumbra not only from Clytemnestra and Deianira but also from Penelope; Philoctetes—whose immobility, cries of pain, and dependence on heroic travelers remind us of Electra—is also feminized in various ways, thus making his own connection to Odysseus's patient wife; Neoptolemus must finally decide whether his model for adult behavior is to be Achilles or Odysseus. The last play brings Sophocles's most famous hero back to the stage, but in a form that aligns him with the protagonists of the two previous dramas in surprising ways and reconfigures the Homeric model of heroism.[4]

Reflection, direct and indirect, on the medium of tragic drama permeates the last three plays. Metatheatrical elements, plays staged within plays, are crucial to the meaning of these works.[5] We see characters put on scenes for each other, usually for the purpose of deception and manipulation. Orestes and his Paedagogus pretend that the former has died in a chariot race so as to lull the Mycenaean royal family into a false sense of safety; in a cruel twist, Electra is unwittingly enlisted in the production, singing a passionate eulogy to an empty urn. Odysseus, Neoptolemus, and the chorus of sailors all perform before Philoctetes, hoping to trick him into delivering his bow to Troy. Polyneices and Antigone act out a tragedy in miniature after the old Oedipus refuses to help his son.

Though hardly a new feature of Sophoclean drama—Athena's sadistic production starring the maddened Ajax opens the earliest extant play (*Aj.* 65–133)—the appearance of metatheatrical elements in works from the last years of the fifth century, when Athenian intellectual life was at the end of a period of rapid and unsettling change, gives them added urgency. New ideas about the sources of human excellence and the implications of these ideas for the distribution of power and status in Athenian society came with the new democratic system. At the root of this ferment was the question of how to evaluate a human life. Should inherited excellence continue to provide the basis for the distribution of social and political leverage, or—as the Sophists and their adherents claimed—could anyone learn to be excellent and thus be a fitting holder of power?[6] When we add in the terrible pressures of an extended war on Athenian society, the interest in how a preeminently public art form functions in that society as a vehicle for dramatizing issues of value becomes yet more intense.[7]

Finally, the Sophoclean tragic hero—lonely, defiant, and self-destructive— undergoes a crucial transformation in the last three plays. The phrase "tragic hero" is so familiar to us now, from so many contexts, that some qualification is necessary here for our purposes. Our understanding of Sophocles's version of this figure must not be contaminated by modern ideas about heroism, which usually imply some measure of approval. A hero in the modern sense is perhaps someone we would like to emulate, perhaps even model ourselves on. Clearly, this paradigm will not fit the protagonists in the extant plays of Sophocles. The particular cluster of traits we will be looking at in this study appears first in Greek literature in the Achilles of the *Iliad*. Two aspects of Homer's creation are especially germane. First, Achilles draws our attention not because he is coura- geous, modest, or compassionate but because he *goes too far*, crosses boundar- ies that define for the Greeks the nature of human existence. He can do so partly because of the facts of his birth, the son of a minor goddess and therefore semi- divine. Such a figure is useful to artists, because he or she can draw our imagi- nation across those crucial boundaries and invite us to think about them, which in turn prompts reflection on the precise nature of human experience and the meaning of a human life. When Achilles launches his final quest for vengeance in Books 20–22 of the poem, he crosses over more than one important bound- ary. Behaving now like a god, now like a wild beast, clogging the flow of the river with corpses, and, ultimately, playing the role of the Death God in Book 24, Achilles is the figure that Homer uses to keep our attention on the boundary between life and death, where much of the meaning of the epic is created.

The second aspect of Achilles's character that Sophocles draws on is a cer- tain kind of temperament. With his egregious abilities come outsized expecta- tions. As we learn in Book 1 of the poem, he considers himself to be the best of the Achaeans at fighting and killing, and thus deserving of the most rewards. When opposed, he flares into anger, fueled by pride. His furious exit from the Greek camp leaves him isolated and leads him to demand that his divine mother compensate for his unjust treatment by calling in a favor from Zeus, ensuring the suffering and death of many of his comrades. He continues to hold himself out of the fighting, despite abject pleas from various comrades in Books 9 and 16, only returning when Patroclus is killed. The combination of stubborn self- ishness, pride, and anger we see in Achilles fuels a defiance of powerful forces that animate the universe, divine will, fate, and, the most important of them, the fact of human mortality. The traits we see in Homer's hero make him destructive, of himself and of those around him. Perhaps the adjective that defines Achilles most accurately is *deinos*, "inspiring awe, fear, astonishment." He is *deinos*, to be treated with great care.[8]

These traits are prominently on display in the heroes of Sophocles's earlier extant plays. Ajax, Antigone, Herakles, and the young Oedipus all defy ultimately invincible forces, bringing misery and often death to themselves and those around them. These characters are defined for us by the exercise of their outsized will. The heroes of Aeschylean and Euripidean drama often display similar characteristics, but only in Sophocles do we see the hero so consistently dominate the action by the exercise of his or her will. The late protagonists show us the same temperament: Electra's stubborn refusal to bend, Philoctetes's lonely suffering and resistance to the commands of the oracle, the defiant old Oedipus, railing and cursing. The "heroic temper," as Bernard Knox defined it in his brilliant study, remains consistent throughout these plays.[9] But as we will see, each of the heroes in the last three plays is positioned in the larger context of the drama so as to present a new paradigm for the hero's agency and relationship to higher forces. Having created vivid realizations of a perspective that begins with Homer's Achilles, Sophocles now reimagines his heroes and by so doing opens up the possibilities of the genre just as it comes to an end in Athens.

Much of the difficulty—and the interest—in the last three plays comes from Sophocles's distancing of the protagonist from the central heroic action of the drama.[10] Orestes and the Paedagogus arrive at the royal palace and proceed, with ruthless efficiency, to carry out the murders, while Electra stands aside and reacts emotionally to events. Since the focus of the first eight hundred lines is almost exclusively on her and those with whom she argues, a gap opens up onstage between the mythical action and the hero. Philoctetes too is set apart from the act required by the oracle, the return of Herakles's bow (and the return of the disabled hero himself) to Troy. Mired in his pain and loneliness, he is necessary to the divine purposes that inform the myth but not an active agent. In each case, we are encouraged to view the imperatives of the old story from a slightly oblique perspective, affording some detachment from them.

The displacement of the hero continues in *Oedipus at Colonus*, and is if anything more overt. Again, others need the protagonist to complete the actions of the myth but he remains apart. Various others come to the old man and try to use him to effect their plans. Creon wants him to return to the vicinity of

Thebes, so the city can try to control the power the oracles have predicted will emanate from his grave. Polyneices asks for his blessing—again in response to an oracle—so that he can prevail in his fight with Eteocles over the throne of Thebes. Oedipus remains aloof from the urgencies of both, and in the end marches off toward a third destiny also foretold in oracles. The scene between Oedipus and his son is particularly telling. Receiving a curse instead of a blessing, Polyneices trudges back to Thebes and certain death. His decision to return completes the dynamic so common in tragic stories, where the hero chooses death to avoid shame. We and Oedipus, meanwhile, look on from a distance.

This built-in detachment from the myths, combined with metatheatrical elements, suggests that Sophocles, like other artists and intellectuals in the later fifth century, was perhaps beginning to question the usefulness of the old myths for responding to problems of his own time. As our attention is drawn insistently toward the suffering and emotional warping that events have exacted from Electra, so our confidence that the triumph of Orestes will heal her wanes; Troy and its imperatives seem far away as we witness Philoctetes's misery and the cynical manipulations of his visitors; the mysterious and powerful disappearance of Oedipus into the company of the gods, with all of its existential and religious implications, makes the back-story from the Theban cycle seem small, more a matter of sibling rivalry than cosmic import. Though Sophocles continues to develop his art form through the last plays, we also see some retrospection in their scrutiny of traditional sources of truth. Large questions arise from the plays about the ways that Sophocles and his fellow artists gave access to and reflect on reality through their art.

The confluence of endings that accompanies Sophocles's last works, of Athenian democracy, tragic drama, and, of course, of the playwright's own life, creates for those plays a tantalizing context: the last work composed by a ninety-year-old playwright focuses on an old man's final day on earth, ending with a mysterious death in the very place where the artist was born; the three plays composed in the last decade of the author's life reflect insistently on the medium through which he refracted the reality in which he lived; this medium reached its zenith alongside the new democracy invented by Athens, in which Sophocles himself took an active part, a system that necessarily challenged deeply held beliefs about the contours of human life.

By contrast with this suggestive matrix, the facts about Sophocles's life in Athens are few and not particularly illuminating.[11] He was apparently a respected artist, soldier, and citizen, but beyond that we know little. Yet the *lives* dramatized in his surviving plays, seen through the prism of myth, history, and artistic form, are rich and suggestive: male and female, young, middle-aged, and very old. We will not be constructing here any kind of biography of the artist from the work. We will however give ourselves permission to reflect on the arc of human experience represented in the final three plays, which continues to evolve right up until Oedipus walks through the doors of the *skēnē*, into the grove of the Eumenides, off the Athenian stage and out of this world.

In the reading that follows, we will be tracing the evolution of Sophocles's paradigm for the tragic hero through his last three plays. Doing so will require some balancing of perspectives. We will address each play as a dramatic and artistic whole, focusing at times on details of dramaturgy—where we see Sophocles developing and perfecting his mastery of the form as a vehicle for expressing new ideas—but also tracking the use of larger patterns of action that link the plays to major themes in Greek literature. We will be looking back to Sophocles's artistic sources in Greek literature, especially Homeric epic and Athenian tragedy. At the same time, we will try to define and follow, through the various continuities between the heroes of these late works, the emergence of a new understanding of the Sophoclean tragic hero. We will conclude by considering how this emerging figure might reflect both the historical context of the dramas, the last years of the Peloponnesian War, and the final years of the playwright's long and fruitful life.

CHAPTER 2

Electra

Glory Bathed in Tears

My child, my child, you have
chosen a glorious life bathed in tears.

(Sophocles's *Electra* 1085–86)

The prologue of *Electra* is all about men and their imperatives. Orestes, Pylades (a silent character), and the Paedagogus (Orestes's childhood tutor) enter and stand in front of the central doors of the *skēnē*, here the entrance to the royal palace at Mycenae. It is, the old man proclaims, the place Orestes has longed to see:

Oh child of Agamemnon who once led the army
at Troy, here, now, you can look upon
what you've always wanted to see.
This is ancient Argos, the place for which you've yearned,
the grove of Inachus' daughter, stung by the gadfly.

(1–5)

The description continues for another nine lines, but we know where we are. The mythical revenge story is underway. As we enter this heroic milieu, compound epithets add an epic flavor: *oistroplēgos*, "gadfly-stung" (5), *lukoktonou*, "wolf-killing" (6), *poluchrusous*, "rich in gold" (9), *poluphthoron*, "destruction-filled" (10).[1] The revenge story carries its own imperatives: Orestes must avenge his father's murder; decisive action is needed; no time for hesitation.

7

In his reply, Orestes takes up the mantle of the noble aristocratic son. His "dearest of retainers" is like a well-bred horse, old but still full of heart, pricking up his ears. Orestes, should he go astray, can count on the old boy for support and advice. Next, a brisk narrative of his trip to Apollo's shrine at Delphi, the oracle's instructions, and Orestes's plans for carrying them out. The Paedagogus, disguised as a Phocian, is to be the advance man, planting a false story about Orestes's death in a chariot race, spying out the situation in the palace. He ends with a prayer to the gods for success: may he win riches and put his ancestral house in order. He urges the old man on to his appointed tasks. Prompt action is needed (50–76).

An anguished cry from offstage breaks the momentum. The Paedagogus thinks it might be a slave from the palace. Orestes wonders if could be the unfortunate Electra—should they stay and listen? To this, an emphatic "no" from the old slave: lingering to listen to a woman's distress would take up precious time and distract the avengers from their heroic deeds. Nothing must come before their mission, which starts with a libation at the grave of Agamemnon. That way lie victory and power. They exit quickly and leave an empty stage (77–85).[2]

The epic coloring of the language in these lines, the simile of horse-breeding, and the hypercompetitive chariot race all blend well with the mythical story, driven along by the need for fame, *kleos*, and the status it conveys in the masculine heroic world. The revenge plot demands not only prompt action but precise timing. The Greek word *kairos*, the base meaning of which is "due measure" or "right proportion," appears three times in the prologue. When applied to the concept of time, the word overlaps with *akmē*, both meaning the right time for action, the critical moment.[3] The Paedagogus insists that there is no time for hesitation (*oknein kairos*); the moment for action (*ergōn akmē*) is at hand (22). Orestes trusts the old man to keep him from missing the *kairos* (31) of the occasion; the two of them must move now: "So we both will be off. This is the right moment (*kairos*), /the chief determinant of every deed for men" (75–76).

While efficiently launching the revenge plot, Orestes lets slip a few potentially disquieting details. Apollo's oracle instructs him to get his revenge through "trickery" (*doloisi*, 37), not the direct, manly method favored by most masculine heroes. Though the Homeric Odysseus offers a powerful precedent for using deceit in a heroic cause, by the late fifth century that figure had come to have a much more problematic ethical profile in Athenian drama.[4] Trickery was of course part of the traditional story, but Sophocles's Orestes seems to be intent here on attributing the deceit to Apollo, as if to head off criticism of his methods. In any event, we will see that this aspect of Orestes's behavior will have a significant afterlife in Sophocles's last two plays.

Yet more troubling are Orestes's reflections on his false death:

> For what harm can come to me, when I die in word (*logōi*)
> but am saved in fact (*ergoisi*) and can win glory?
> I think that no word (*pēma*) that brings you gain (*kerdei*) is bad.
> For I know that many times wise men
> have died in fiction. Then, when they return home
> again, they receive honor all the more.
> Just so, I glory in knowing that from this story
> I shall, alive, shine on my enemies like a star.

> (59–66)

The polarity of *logos/ergon*, "word/deed," was a potent site for debate in fifth century Athenian intellectual life.[5] To explore the relationship between the two terms is to confront, implicitly or explicitly, the connections between perception and reality, a topic that had drawn the attention of both philosophers and literary artists from Homer onward. On the level of politics, the debate touched on vital issues in the emerging democracy of Athens. The wider distribution of political power in the new democratic government had already challenged aristocratic ideas about the sources of human excellence. If family membership—and thus blood relationships—were not to be the primary basis for holding and exercising power in the polis, how was fitness for such duties to be measured and acquired? This question and others like it animated the thinking of intellectuals, and particularly the Sophists—traveling teachers who spoke in Athens in the mid- to late fifth century. New ideas about the role of education in the formation of human character—that one could learn to be excellent, as opposed to the claim that excellence was something innate, transmitted by blood—lay at the center of the intellectual agenda of these teachers and were viewed with suspicion by more traditional thinkers.[6] Like Achilles in his response to Odysseus in Book 9 of the *Iliad*, the latter group would "hate like the gates of Hades the man who hides one thing in his mind and says another" (*Iliad* 9. 312–13).

As one who presented plays in the open, democratic venue of a civic religious festival, Sophocles would presumably need at least to acknowledge popular views, which would view with suspicion the claim of *logos* always to represent truth.[7] Orestes has already introduced the issues earlier when saying that they can tell the royal couple the "pleasant story" of his death and cremation, thus deceiving them with words (*logōi*, 56). Though Apollo has instructed him to use deceit, Orestes seems to be warming to the assignment in ways that cast some doubt on his heroic credentials. As the play progresses, we will see the *logos/ergon* polarity surface several times, in ways that make it an important part of the fabric of Sophocles's dramatic vision.

Enter Electra

Once the men have cleared the stage, Electra enters through the central doors, delivering a solo lament of some thirty-four lines. Her impassioned tone changes the atmosphere onstage immediately.[8] Conversational iambic trimeters give way to anapests, a meter associated with a chorus' entrance song; in place of the men's brisk plotting, driven by urgencies in the mythical story, we enter an impressionistic world where time passes slowly, punctuated by the cyclical rhythms of nature:[9]

> Oh holy light
> and air with equal share of earth, how many
> songs of grief, how many blows against my breast
> have you heard, whenever murky night has been
> left behind?

(86–91)

Electra alone continues to mourn her father's treacherous murder at the hands of her mother and Aegisthus, and will not cease so long as she lives. She compares herself to Procne: she has become a nightingale who mourns a lost loved one.[10] She concludes with a prayer to chthonic gods of the underworld—Hades, Persephone, Hermes, guide of souls to the underworld—and finally *Ara*, "curse," and the Erinyes, goddesses of vengeance who punish crimes against blood relatives. These last creatures play a prominent role in the *Oresteia*, hounding Orestes after the matricide. Here they are invoked to avenge a crime against the marriage bed, an unusual role for them.[11] As the play goes on, Electra herself will sometimes be identified with the Erinyes, as she pursues vengeance against her own mother.[12]

The chorus, made up of adult Argive women, has entered the orchestra for the first time while Electra is speaking and begins to sing at line 121. We expect a choral song, divided into pairs of metrically corresponding stanzas, strophes followed by antistrophes, called the "parodos," or "entrance song," the usual way a chorus comes onstage for the first time in an Athenian tragedy. Instead, Electra sings in response to the chorus, sharing each of the three strophes and three antistrophes, the meter of her lines replicating the chorus' exactly (a formal device called "metrical corresponsion"), then ending the parodos with a solo in the epode (235–50).[13] This kind of lyrical dialogue appears here first in extant Sophoclean tragedy as a replacement for the usual choral parodos.[14] One effect of this new form is to emphasize the sympathetic connection between Electra and these women. As the play progresses, they will come to be the lonely princess's only support.[15]

Though the women sympathize with Electra's grief, they try gently to convince her to let go of grieving for her father. Clytemnestra's hand in the murder was evil, and she deserves to perish, but some moderation in grief is best. Electra will not, in any event, raise Agamemnon up again from his grave by weeping or prayers. Her sorrow is great, but she is not alone: her siblings—Chrysothemis, Iphiannasa, and Orestes—all share the pain of losing their father. Orestes is sure to return, with Zeus's help, and will avenge the murder. Meanwhile, she should turn her grief over to Zeus, who rules all things. Time is a gentle god, and her patience will be rewarded. She must speak no more of her sorrows. By doing so, she falls into evils of her own making, breeding wars in her soul. She must endure and should not struggle against those in power (121–220).

Electra's response to the women is respectful but firm. She calls them "the offspring of nobles" (*genethla gennaiōn*, 129), who have come to comfort her. She knows and understands what they are saying, yet she is unwilling to give up grieving for her father. She begs them to let her "wander" (*aluein*, 135). Those who forget the pitiful death of parents are fools. She keeps before us as models both Procne and Niobe, mothers who lost their children (145–52). She herself is childless and alone, with no bridegroom to protect her. Orestes, meanwhile, does nothing, answering none of her messages (164–72; 185–92). The day of Agamemnon's murder was the most hateful of all to her, and that night, "the terrible pain of an unspeakable feast." May the murderers suffer in return (202–12).

This first exchange between Electra and the chorus is critical for our understanding of the princess and her position in the drama. Unlike the male elders in the chorus of *Antigone*, who side with Creon until the end of the play, or the young girls in *The Women of Trachis*, who are too naïve and inexperienced to offer much help to Deianira, the support of these women adds some legitimacy to Electra's claims. They are apparently mature, from worthy families, have lived life and endured pain themselves, and can speak with authority on such things. Comparing themselves to a caring mother (233–35), they begin from a position of sympathy with Electra's anger and grief, sharing her outrage at the murders, but also see the wisdom of accepting limits on the expression of emotion in a world controlled by the royal family. Most importantly, despite their sympathy, they see Electra's pain as finally self-inflicted. Instead of children, she "breeds" (*tiktous'*) wars in herself (218).

Electra seems to grant this last point, saying that she understands and respects their position, but must persist anyway. In this stance she echoes all of Sophocles's earlier heroes, who are defined by their self-destructive refusal to budge in defiance of powers ultimately beyond their control. In other words, Sophocles points here to Electra as the hero of the play.[16] While this gesture may seem unremarkable to us now in hindsight, it would certainly have been a striking innovation when the play was first produced. The contemporary Athenian audience would expect Orestes, not Electra, to be the hero of this revenge story. He certainly fills this role in earlier versions of the story, Homer's *Odyssey* and in Aeschylus's version of the myth, *The Libation Bearers*.[17] Although Orestes has launched—amid all the masculine trappings—the traditional revenge plot in the prologue, he is an unlikely candidate for a Sophoclean tragic hero. He acts out his role in the myth with straightforward efficiency, but his character is relatively uncomplicated, a can-do male in whom the tortured inner struggles typical of Sophocles's heroes simply do not appear.[18] Rather, once the spotlight shifts to Electra and her suffering, Orestes and his plot (and indeed all the male characters) disappear from the stage for over five hundred lines. The revenge plot seems to go underground, a stream running along silently while the emotional fireworks go off onstage.[19]

By separating his hero from direct involvement in the revenge plot, Sophocles opens up a space between the myth and the story his play tells. This tactic in turn fosters in us as audience a certain detachment from the mythical story and its imperatives. We will see that Sophocles proceeds from this point to develop a new trajectory for his dramas, one which he will continue to pursue and enrich through his last two plays.

The Woman Who Waits

What then, we may ask, is the heroic task toward which Electra directs her energies? To wait, to endure, to refuse to be silenced.[20] The chorus and others will urge her to let go of her anger and move on, but she will not do so. She waits for Orestes to release her from what she sees as the bondage imposed on her by Clytemnestra and Aegisthus. As a woman who waits for men to return, Electra recalls several female characters in Greek literature. In a patriarchal culture permeated by war, the woman left behind by soldiers would be a potent figure in the imagination of artists and the source of some anxiety. Will a wife remain faithful or give in to the advances of other men? Does her abandonment in the service of masculine imperatives foster anger and resentment in her? What welcome awaits the warrior returning from battle? Homeric epic provides the first vivid examples. Andromache in the *Iliad* models the perfect wife, loving and patient, crushed by the loss of her husband, with Helen as the dark counterexample. Penelope also remains faithful, though her portrait is perhaps more ambiguous,[21] while Clytemnestra is irredeemably bad. This latter character makes a riveting return in Aeschylus's *Oresteia* and the two other extant Electra plays. Sophocles's Deianira offers a softer alternative, patient and forgiving, even in the face of Herakles's womanizing. Finally, Euripides explores the dynamic from a characteristically oblique angle in his *Helen* and *Iphigenia in Tauris*.

Comparing Sophocles's Electra to other realizations of the type is revealing. Only she and her sister Iphigenia are virgins, waiting for a brother rather than a husband. Whereas Iphigenia and Deianira are both at least outwardly loyal to the males who have betrayed them and maintain a seemly patience in the face of their abandonment, Electra's resentment and pain are evident and definitive for her character. Locating her on the continuum of "good" and "bad" women is challenging. As one who suffers in the absence of a male, she is close to Penelope and Deianira. Yet her demeanor, expressing anger and pain loudly and often, puts off both her oppressors and her supporters. The latter fear for her safety if she persists in defying the rulers; according to both groups, she is noisier than she ought to be. These supposed defects will be dramatized at length in her exchanges with Chrysothemis and Clytemnestra.

More important than any of these similarities and differences is the fact that Sophocles's Electra, unlike any other example of this type of character, is positioned as the hero of her play.[22] Admirable as are both Penelope and Deianira,

both finally give place to males playing the heroic role (however problemati-
cally, in the case of Herakles). Aeschylus's Clytemnestra is a powerful figure, to
be sure. Indeed, part of the energy of his *Agamemnon* is generated by her usurping of the male role in the royal palace. But Agamemnon is the hero of the first
play of the *Oresteia* and Orestes steps into that role in the last two. By present-
ing Electra as the hero of his play, Sophocles sets himself a challenge. Though
the character has in one sense many antecedents, as we have seen, for her to be
the focal point of the drama while not being an active agent in the revenge plot
creates a curious disjunction.[23] Instead of watching Orestes pursuing retribution, we are invited to consider the impact of events on Electra, to look at the
myth from her perspective, at an oblique angle. By structuring his play in this
way, the playwright invites reflection on the efficacy of both the old story and
the art form of tragic drama as vehicles for examining urgent issues arising
from the events of the story.

Heroic Resistance

Electra and the chorus revert to iambic trimeters at line 250 and continue their
exchange for another seventy-five or so lines. Though they have urged restraint,
the older women affirm their support:

> I have come, daughter, urging my interests
> and also yours. If I speak wrongly, press on,
> for I will follow you.
>
> (251–53)

In response to their support, Electra expresses shame at grieving too much. But
a strong necessity forces her to act in this way. She cannot look on the suffering
in her father's house, growing like an evil plant rather than diminishing, and do
nothing; her relations with Clytemnestra are "most hateful" (262), and she is
forced to share a house with her father's murderers, a prisoner whose move-
ments they control; they may imagine how the days pass for her, seeing Aegisthus sitting on her father's throne, dressed in his robes, pouring libations on the
hearth where he killed Agamemnon; and worst of all, their "final outrage" (271),
sex in her father's bed. Clytemnestra taunts her; Orestes never comes, leaving
her to die in her misery. In the midst of all this, what is the point of good sense
or piety? Surrounded by evil, one must practice evil (254–309).

Electra builds her case for a kind of passive resistance here, though her last claim, that in the presence of evil she must pursue it herself, leaves open the possibility of a more active stance in the future. Further refining of her position in the household and in the play now follows, as her sister Chrysothemis enters. The exchange that follows is clearly modeled to some degree on the conflict between Antigone and Ismene, a conventional and timid young woman serving as foil to her more assertive sister.[24] Chrysothemis, like the chorus, is worried that Electra's open expression of anger and pain will bring punishment from the royal couple. This threat has been enough to keep the younger sister quiet. While she feels pain over the present troubles, she has no power over the rulers, and if she wants to remain free, she must obey them. She hopes that Electra will do the same (328–40).

Electra's answer reintroduces the polarity of *logos/ergon*. How can Chrysothemis forget her father while honoring her mother? She rejects her sister's claim that she has no power to show how much she hates the king and queen:

> You yourself said just now that if you had
> the power, you would show your hatred for them.
> But when I do everything to honor my father,
> you do not join me in this work (*ksunerdeis*, from the same root as *ergon*)
> but try to turn me from it.
>
> (347–50)

Does this, she demands, not add the charge of cowardice to her present troubles? Electra still lives, albeit miserably, and by giving her enemies pain she at least honors the dead. Chrysothemis says she hates the royal couple in words (*logōi*, 357), but in her actions (*ergōi*, 358) she agrees with them. The distinction that Orestes raised rather breezily in the prologue takes on a darker tone here. He sees no dishonor in dying in words, as long as he can triumph in fact over his enemies; Electra cannot abide her sister hating in words but acting as if she acquiesces in the tyranny.[25]

The difference is instructive. Electra's insistence on the need for integrity in both word and action, expressed in the midst of her passionate speech, freights her claims with a moral seriousness that contrasts tellingly with Orestes's blithe tone. Electra sees her sister as a hypocrite and a coward. Where would that leave Orestes in her (and our) estimation? The tone of the prologue tends to gloss over any moral ambiguity in Orestes's approach—swift action is paramount there, with the worthy goal of revenge carrying all before it. Now, seen through the prism of Electra's endless suffering, his words come under a sterner standard and begin to look more slippery. Electra, meanwhile, stakes out ever more firmly the unbending stance of the tragic hero, increasingly isolated from those who love her.[26] Chrysothemis and Orestes are both diminished as moral agents in the light of Electra's principled resistance, while she moves yet further into lonely and painful nobility.

Looking back at Orestes's character through Electra's exchange with her sister raises further questions. Electra condemns by implication her brother's view of the connection between *logos* and *ergon*.[27] In doing so, she establishes herself as the champion of an older, traditional heroic perspective that demands consistency in word and deed. Chrysothemis says that she agrees with Electra but cannot act against the tyrants because she lacks power. Electra restates this dilemma as a failure to harmonize action (*ergon*) with words (*logos*). She herself is not, in her view, guilty of that failure—even though she does not take action but waits for Orestes—since she is openly defiant in word, whatever the consequences. Her sense of herself as serving the cause of justice depends on seeing *her* words as the moral equivalent of *acts*, we might say—Chrysothemis, she says, does not "join her in her work" (349).[28] But at the same time she looks to Orestes to take revenge on the royal couple and save her from her misery. He represents to her the instrument by which her words can become actions. And yet his nobility is in question, since he is content to lie as long as it paves the way for action that brings about a just result. The ironies generated here will only increase as the play progresses.

The chorus now anxiously intervenes, begging the sisters to avoid anger. There is "profit" (*kerdos*, 370) in the words (*logois*) of both, and each could learn from the other. Orestes resurfaces here, as the chorus' advice echoes his confident assertion: "I think that no word (*pēma*) that brings profit is bad" (61). The chorus foresees a different kind of "profit" than did Orestes. He understands *kerdos* as representing the end result of a transaction, which may require some deceit along the way. He dismisses any qualms about the process, which he sees as only "words." For the chorus, the profit is in the words, or more specifically, in the process by which each woman may learn from the words of the other: how the two women behave toward one another can be good for them both.

In the perspective of the prologue, with its emphasis on goal-oriented action, precise timing, and speed, "profit" is understood as the right outcome. To the Greeks, males were the agents of civilization, acting to impose order on the powerful forces of nature. They make human history thereby, and their doing so is preserved in heroic myth. Associated with light and reason, males look upward to the Olympian gods for their guidance and inspiration. In this perspective, time is primarily linear, marking progress toward the creation of human civilization. Thus, Orestes receives his guidance from Apollo, the Olympian god of light and reason, and must be sure to carry out the god's instructions in a timely way, with divine will reinforcing human desire for revenge.

Since Electra's entrance, the stage has been filled exclusively with women, and our view of the events changes. Time, which appeared in the prologue as *kairos*, now slows, settling into endless repetitive cycles: night, day, winter, summer, always circling back to that terrible day when Agamemnon was murdered, the event that ended Electra's happiness and began her imprisonment.[29] The Greeks saw women as closer to the forces of nature than men, their bodies ruled by monthly cycles.[30] Time in this mode of experience is circular, ahistorical. The mythical parallels Electra draws are to women doomed to endless grief, not heroes moving in time toward a desired event within human culture. The chorus urges Electra to turn her anger over to Zeus, who sees all and rules all; time (*chronos*), they say, is a "gentle god" (*eumarēs theos*, 179). The Greek adjective literally means "with a helpful/gentle hand," a soothing companion for long suffering. Women, tied to the forces of nature, less able than men to control their own emotions by reason, become part of what must be controlled and shaped by the hand of males as they create and preserve human civilization. Electra is to give up control and wait for Orestes, who, like Hades, does not "turn his attention away" (*aperitropos*, 182).

The emotional exchange continues as Chrysothemis reveals that if Electra does not quiet down, the royal couple plan to send her out of the country to a dark underground prison, where she will no longer see the light of the sun. There she will "sing [her] evils" (382). All of this will happen as soon as Aegisthus comes home. This dismal prospect confirms the distinctions we have noted above: Aegisthus, the male agent, will silence his stepdaughter by putting her in a dark cave, where she will give endless voice to her "evils" (*kaka*), like Antigone and those dangerous Homeric singers, Calypso and Circe. Electra is undaunted: let him come soon, so she may be away from her tormentors and their collaborators. Chrysothemis keeps trying to make her sister see that subservience to those in power is not cowardice but only good sense, to which Electra replies with typically heroic disdain:

CHRYSOTHEMIS
But honor demands that we not fall into ruin through foolishness.

ELECTRA
I will fall, if I must, honoring my father.

(398–99)

Clytemnestra: The Woman Who Did Not Wait

Chrysothemis gives up trying to convince her sister and starts off to complete the errand that their conversation interrupted, to pour a libation on behalf of Clytemnestra at Agamemnon's grave. Beginning here and continuing for almost four hundred lines, our attention is drawn ever more insistently to Electra's mother.[31] Up to this point, Clytemnestra has been present for us as part of the royal couple, the oppressors of Electra. Now the playwright brings her forward, famous since Homer's *Odyssey* as the supreme example of a faithless wife and treacherous murderer. Having made Electra into the dominant figure in his play, Sophocles draws here on the mythical charge attached to her mother to build our interest in anticipation of the inevitable confrontation to come. Clytemnestra, it seems, has had a disturbing dream:

CHRYSOTHEMIS
The story is that she dreamed of meeting again
your father and mine, who had come again
into the world of light. Then the staff, which he
once carried and now is wielded by Aegisthus,
he took and planted in the earth. From it then
bloomed a fruitful shoot, which overshadowed
the entire land of the Mycenaeans.

(417–24)

In response to this ominous vision, the queen has sent Chrysothemis to the grave as her surrogate. Electra is appalled and demands that her sister throw away the offerings, substituting locks of hair from both of them, plus Electra's girdle. Not only does she want to enlist Agamemnon on the side of his avengers, but the gift of her girdle also adds a sexual charge to the conflict with Clytemnestra: she is her mother's rival for Agamemnon's attention not only at the grave but in his bed.[32] Chrysothemis is to pray for aid from the dead king against their enemies, for themselves and for Orestes. Surely Agamemnon himself sent the dream. Chrysothemis exits to perform the sacrifice, leaving Electra onstage with the chorus, which now sings its first stasimon, or complete song.

In its short song—strophe, antistrophe, and epode—the chorus keeps the focus on Clytemnestra by responding to her dream. As if in answer to her impending presence, they conjure two powerful female figures, "prophetic Justice" (*promantis Dika*, 475–76) and "many-footed, many-handed Erinys, who hides in a secret ambush" (489–91). The former will come to the children's aid and in no long space of time (*ou makrou chronou*); no prophecy is to be found in dreadful dreams if this latter phantom of the night finds no fulfillment. In the epode, they turn their attention and ours to the dark past of the family, recalling the "painful horsemanship" of Pelops, grandfather of Agamemnon, when he won his bride by fixing a chariot race against his prospective father-in-law, Oenomaus, bribing and then killing the latter's charioteer. Now Orestes's plan to deceive the royal couple with the false report of a lethal chariot race becomes part of a pattern of duplicity that spans three generations, the latest version of painful horsemanship, a "torment of many troubles" (515). As the display of female force is about to reach its crescendo in the appearance of Clytemnestra, Sophocles makes sure we remember the masculine plotting that opened the play.

The playwright has made us wait for Clytemnestra, bringing her before us gradually, through Electra's account of her own suffering at the hands of her jailors, Chrysothemis's anxious reporting, and finally the chorus' conjuring of suitably powerful opponents. In the event, she does not disappoint, launching a nasty offensive with her first words to Electra:

> You are wandering around loose again, it seems.
> Aegisthus, who always used to keep you from
> shaming your family—at least outside the house—isn't here.
>
> (516–18)

Unlike the sympathetic women of the chorus, the queen will not allow her daughter to "wander" (cf. *aluein*, 135). Her self-defense comes in the form of an attack: Electra shows her no respect in Aegisthus's absence, telling others she is insolent and unjust, that she arrogantly abuses her; *she* is not arrogant, but only responds in kind to Electra's abuse; yes, she killed Agamemnon, but Justice was also his killer, he who sacrificed his own daughter. And for whose sake? The Argives? They had no right to sacrifice what was hers. Why not offer up one of Menelaus's children? These were the acts of a foolish and evil father! If she seems to think badly, Electra should acquire a just judgment before attacking others (516–51).

Electra aims to refute these charges. Clytemnestra did not act justly in killing her father. Rather, she was persuaded by the evil man she lives with. It was to placate Artemis, not Menelaus, that Agamemnon sacrificed Iphigenia, to effect release from Aulis for the Argives. But even if he did so to help his brother, did he deserve to die for it? By what law (*nomos*, 579)? Clytemnestra should take care that by establishing such a law she not condemn herself. If a life is to be taken for a life, she should die first. And is she not behaving shamefully, begetting children by the man who helped kill her husband, while throwing out the pious children born from a pious union? She acts more like a tyrant than a mother, visiting suffering and torment on Electra, while Orestes languishes in exile. Let her call Electra evil or loud-mouthed or full of shamelessness; if she is so, she comes by it naturally, a child worthy of Clytemnestra (558–608).

Most of the arguments on both sides are familiar from earlier treatments of the myth.[33] The facts of the family history are not in dispute. The struggle we see here is all about how to evaluate the actions. On whose side is justice (*dikē*)? Whom do the gods favor? In Aeschylus's trilogy, these questions are played out against a vast cosmic backdrop, and their resolution in the third play reflects the earlier playwright's optimistic view of the place of Athenian democracy in the larger context of the universe as the Greeks understood it. Because the acts of Aeschylus's characters carry meaning primarily as a reflection of each one's status or role in the family and household of Agamemnon, rather than as individualized persons with recognizable psychological traits, the conflict of moral values can be dramatized more cleanly than in this play, whereas Sophocles has created characters whose interior life and past history complicate our understanding of motive and causation.[34] Though each of these women fields the requisite arguments, the dispute is colored by a complex range of emotions on both sides. Electra embarrasses her mother by her shameful behavior. She is too loud, wandering around saying bad things about the royal couple. Her presence in the palace reminds the queen of her past, and no matter how fiercely she proclaims herself to be just, we suspect that Electra is a source of guilt. Her daughter, meanwhile, knows she is behaving badly and is ashamed of it: "I know that I act wrongly for one my age and against my nature" (617–18). As an unmarried virgin, she cannot fulfill the role usually allotted to women, to provide children. She says that she is forced to act that way against her will because of her mother's hostility. Worst of all, she sees herself as being like her mother.[35]

We might expect this scene, which we have seen Sophocles building toward for hundreds of lines, to take us to the heart of the old story the play dramatizes. The cycle of violence and retaliation raises questions about the nature of justice, the role of the gods in human affairs, the duties of family members to each other. The very depth of the characters Sophocles has created, however, makes it impossible for him to present definitive answers.[36] His Electra, at once powerfully realized and tantalizingly complex, carries too much emotional baggage to be an agent in a cleanly articulated resolution to the family's pain. Clytemnestra, as the character is presented here, in conflict with this Electra, also acts amid crosscurrents of emotions, guilt, anger, shame. This scene is indeed the climax of a dramatic movement that began with Electra's entrance, but we will not find clear answers here to the large questions the revenge story generates. Instead, by bringing Electra together with these different dramatic foils—her sister, the sympathetic older women in the chorus, and finally her mother—the playwright has created a deeper, more complex version of the traditional character from the myth.

Electra is Sophocles's hero in the play, and yet she emerges for us as a fully rounded character out of a dramatic context completely separated from the mechanics of the revenge plot, a world of women who look on as men act. No male character has walked the stage since Orestes and the Paedagogus left it, presumably to refine their plans for the murders. In their absence, we have watched Sophocles create a character whose central traits—stubborn defiance of more powerful forces, a willingness to die rather than be shamed—echo those of his other tragic heroes. The arena for her heroic exertions, however, is entirely emotional and inward, a territory quite different from that of an Oedipus or an Ajax.[37] The questions Sophocles might address here have more to do with how a woman survives when males are occupied elsewhere. Endurance, not timing, *chronos*, rather than *kairos*, will determine outcomes in this world. In what does honorable behavior consist for a woman like Electra? What does she contribute to the good of her city? By orchestrating his play to point toward questions such as these, Sophocles is not only entering new territory as the teller of heroic tales; he is also addressing the nature of those old stories as responses to what besets Athens in his own time. In the next part of the play, we will see him turning his lens on the medium of tragic drama.

Meanwhile, Back at the Palace

The argument between mother and daughter can have no fruitful resolution, and Clytemnestra ends it by turning to pray to Apollo, whose statue is onstage. As if in answer, the Paedagogus—one of the god's agents in the play—appears. He says he has "pleasant words" (*logous/hēdeis*, 666–67) for the royal couple from a friend, the king of the Phocians:

CLYTEMNESTRA
What sort of business, stranger? Tell me. I know well
you come from a friend, and will say friendly words.

PAEDAGOGUS
To put it briefly, Orestes is dead.

ELECTRA
Oh, I am ruined! This is the day I die.

CLYTEMNESTRA
What are you saying, sir? Don't listen to her.

PAEDAGOGUS
I have said and say again, Orestes is dead.

ELECTRA
Oh misery, I am destroyed. I live no more.

CLYTEMNESTRA
You, keep to yourself. Stranger, tell me the truth,
How did he die?

(671–79)

The old slave brings the revenge plot back onstage after an interval of nearly six hundred lines, reminding us of its built-in urgencies. Things will get moving again, we feel. Electra, who has been so commanding in her heroic resistance, is elbowed out of the way by the queen, reduced in an instant to abject impotence. The Paedagogus now launches into a gripping account of how Orestes was killed in a chariot race at Delphi. The story, over eighty lines long, brings back the epic flavor of the prologue, as the old man recreates the great race, the noble contestants listed in a catalogue strongly reminiscent of Homeric epic. His account of the race itself recalls the funeral games for Patroclus in Book 23 of the *Iliad*.[38]

It is, of course, all lies. The *logos/ergon* polarity returns here, its ironies intact. The Paedagogus, masculine agent of deeds, uses his "sweet words" to further the revenge plot. All the words that passed between mother and daughter in the suffocating shadow of the palace, freighted with genuine and wrenching emotions, have achieved nothing except to harden the two sides in their views. Now this false tale of heroic deeds supposedly done far away drains all the life from the genuinely heroic Electra. Like that of its predecessor two generations before, the outcome of this chariot race depends on deceit. Orestes, the Paedagogus proudly announces, first entered the footrace as a "brilliant" (*lampros*, 685) figure. He won, making the outcome of that race equal to his "appearance" (*phusei*, 686). The word *phusis* here has an ironic double meaning. It can refer to someone's outward appearance, but it carries with it the idea of "inborn nature." So here, the word fits with the old slave's glowing portrait of Orestes as heroic victor, but also hints at the darker view of Orestes's inner nature reflected in his use of deceit, the legacy of Pelops.[39] The slave continues:

So as to tell much in a few words,
I do not know of the powerful deeds of such a man.

(688–89)

These words can mean that the speaker knows no man equal to Orestes, but could just as easily—and more straightforwardly—mean that the man these words describe does not exist.

The old slave's news has the desired effect of lulling Clytemnestra into a false sense of security. As Orestes predicted in the prologue, by dying in fiction (*logōi*, 59) he now shines (*lampsein*) on his enemies like a star (66). The queen does express some ambivalence about her son's death: "Oh Zeus, what of these things? Should I call them fortunate or terrible yet profitable (*kerdē*)" (766–67)? Are Clytemnestra's sentiments genuine, or is she putting on a false show of remorse for the visitor? Given the naturalism of the preceding argument between mother and daughter, with its undercurrent of unexpressed feelings, we might well take what the queen says at face value. The concept of profit (*kerdos*) surfaces again here, with its varying shades of meaning in the play. Where does profit lie for the queen? Do we hear an echo of Orestes ("I think that no word (*pēma*) that brings you gain (*kerdei*) is bad" [61])? Or is the chorus' formulation (370), stressing sympathetic cooperation, more appropriate? Given the queen's continued abuse of her daughter, the former looks like a better fit for now.

Clytemnestra's reflective mood passes quickly, and she returns to her adversarial stance toward both children. Electra is like a vampire, sucking her very lifeblood (785–86). Orestes, like his father, abandoned her:

> Turning away from my breasts and my nurture, he
> became a foreigner in exile. After he left
> this land, he no longer saw me, but calling me
> the murderer of his father, he threatened to do dreadful things,
> so that sweet sleep covered me neither night or day, but
> time (*chronos*) stood over me like one about to die.
>
> (776–82)

Here is a remarkably different picture of Orestes's departure from Mycenae as an infant than the one we have heard from Electra. The queen calls him an "exile" (*phugas*), who has revolted (*apostas*) from her care. Both words are commonly used of political enemies.[40] In this view, Orestes, even as a baby, was her political rival. Our first reaction is likely to be revulsion: having expressed regret for the death of her child, in the next breath Clytemnestra condemns him as a political enemy. At the same time, we may be prompted to reflect on a parallel between mother and daughter: both are resentful at what they see as abandonment by their male protectors.

In the logic of the myth, Clytemnestra and her daughter must be separated by an implacable enmity: by killing Agamemnon, Clytemnestra forfeited any claim to sympathy from Electra. Orestes, meanwhile, is appropriately seen by the queen as her enemy, a dangerous rival for power. But by staging a more naturalistic confrontation between the two women than in earlier treatments, Sophocles lets us glimpse another perspective, in which mother and daughter are both left to fend for themselves while men pursue glory and power. The prologue's tone of triumphal masculinity has established Orestes as Clytemnestra's enemy and rival, who acts in pursuit of "victory" and "power" (*nikēn* . . .

kratos, 85). But in the world of women on display between the end of the pro-logue and the entrance of the Paedagogus, even Electra sees to her chagrin that she resembles her mother; she too resents the failure of her man to return and protect her.

The motivations inherent in the mythical revenge plot will always be more prominent onstage than submerged, ambiguous emotions like the ones we have been exploring here. Yet the hints that Sophocles gives us of crosscurrents of emotion that do not fit in the traditional account prompt reflection on the story as a vehicle for addressing the issues that arise from it. Electra is a problem for those onstage because she will not be quiet and wait for release from her suffer-ing. She also challenges our perception of the logic of the traditional revenge story. Can such a shattered figure, wracked by competing emotions of rage, re-sentment, and shame, ever be restored in a way that would be true to the prob-ing portrait Sophocles creates? What would "justice" mean to a woman like her? These difficulties will only increase as the play progresses.

The Paedagogus's account of the chariot race interposes another kind of filter into our perception of the play. It becomes on the one hand another piece of the increasingly ironic and complex mosaic of meanings clustered around the polarity of *logos/ergon*: here is an elaborate *logos* that is instrumental within the revenge plot, furthering the *ergon* that Orestes must perform, but entirely false, describing an *ergon* that never happened.[41] At the same time, the report is, as we know, a *performance*, put on to deceive the royal couple. As such, it is part of a drama the conspirators will stage, in which Electra will unwittingly play a part. Now we are offered the chance to think about the medium of tragic drama itself, especially its function as a vehicle for representing human experi-ence.[42] If Orestes and his henchmen can use the medium, itself a mixture of *logoi* and *erga*, to tell strategic lies, what does that say about Athenian tragedy? What exactly is the *ergon* that the plays effect within Athenian society? In a time of war and prolonged suffering, what could Athenian citizens expect to learn about themselves and their lives from going to the theater?[43]

Change Partners and Sing

Clytemnestra and the old slave proceed companionably into the palace at line 803. There follows another long stretch, nearly three hundred lines, in which no male characters appear. Electra reassumes control of the stage, singing and talking with the chorus and Chrysothemis. She begins with a monologue of about twenty lines, rehearsing her sorrows, abandoned now for good by Orestes and willing to die. At line 823, the chorus responds sympathetically, and there begins a lyric dialogue in which Electra and the chorus sing in strophes, as they did in the parodos. Sophocles takes a step further in his choral technique here, as the metrical and grammatical units are divided between actor and chorus, what is called *"antilabē"* in straight dialogue.[44] A sung version of this kind of exchange appears here first in extant Sophoclean drama. As in the parodos, the playwright supplants a traditional choral song with sung dialogue. The effect, as earlier, is to develop Electra's character relationally, her thoughts and feelings bringing an immediate response from the sympathetic older women. Using lyric *antilabē* raises the intensity of the exchange yet further.

The chorus tries to console Electra for her loss by offering a mythical parallel: Amphiarius too was a king murdered after being betrayed by his wife Eriphyle, but he retained his powers in the underworld, unlike other insubstantial ghosts. Electra refutes their example by reminding them that unlike Agamemnon, Amphiarius was avenged by his son Alcmaeon (846–48).[45] This gambit having failed, the chorus falls back on proverbial wisdom: death comes for all mortals. Electra is ready for this attempt at consolation too: does everyone die trampled by horses, entangled in the reins (860–63)? As in their first lyric dialogue, so here Electra will not bend, in spite of the chorus' gentle attempts to comfort her.

Chrysothemis enters excitedly at this point, bringing the happy news that Orestes must be back. Questioned closely, she says that she has found fresh offerings and a lock of Orestes's hair at Agamemnon's tomb. Electra crushes her hopes, telling her of the Paedagogus's report. The offerings must be, she says, from someone else in honor of the dead Orestes. Electra brusquely dismisses her sister's regret at having been wrong, but then surprises us with a new resolve: "That's how things are; but if you will obey me,/ you will lighten the weight of present pain" (938–39). Though ready to die just a moment before, Electra seems to have drawn some small energy from her sister's report. Rather than wasting away in despair, she now contemplates action in the service of revenge. Now that Orestes has died, the two of them must act! Their familial piety will win them renown, in life and in death:

Who of the citizens or strangers, seeing us
will not greet us with praise such as this:

"Look, friends, at these two sisters,
who when their enemies were well established
together saved their ancestral home,
stood up against murder and thought nothing for
their own lives. All should love them, revere them.
Therefore in the festivals and throughout the city
let all honor them for their courage."
Every man will say such things of us,
in life and in death, so our glory (*kleos*) will never die.

(975–85)

Chrysothemis remains afraid of the king and queen, and earns yet more scorn from her sister. The two argue back and forth for another sixty or so lines, the dispute following a familiar pattern, Chrysothemis insisting that to resist those who have more power would be senseless, unwilling to die for glory, Electra scornfully dismissing her caution as cowardice, opting to serve what she sees as justice, *dikē,* regardless of the cost. The chorus intervenes once, nervously urging Electra to relent: nothing brings more profit (*kerdos*) than foresight and wisdom (1015–16).

We are reminded here of the chorus' earlier reference to *kerdos,* also a doomed attempt to effect some cooperation between the sisters. In fact, this echo is only one part of a much larger set of correspondences. The structure of the entire section from the entrance of the old slave to the end of the chorus' second stasimon at line 1097 replicates the first 515 lines of the drama: male plotting, a monologue by Electra, lyric dialogue between the chorus and Electra, argument between the sisters, choral song.[46] Though doubling of individual scenes is fairly common in Sophocles's plays, structural repetition on this scale is unusual and prompts further thought. Metaphors from music seem appropriate here, with repeated narrative (and rhythmic) structures suggesting some kind of aesthetic form, the parallels pointing to comparisons but also contrasts. We note for instance that the parallel sections frame the confrontation between Electra and Clytemnestra, which many have seen as the heart of the play at least in terms of the traditional myth.

At the same time, we may observe that in the second iteration, strict segregation of male and female characters breaks down. After the Paedagogus enters, he seeks out Clytemnestra to deliver his "good news." Electra, meanwhile, hovers at the edge of the ensuing exchange, shoved aside by the queen and ignored by the slave. The heroic authority that Electra's resistance has won her fades away as the male plotting turns our attention—and the trajectory of the play—toward the goals of the revenge myth again. *Kairos*, not *chronos*, will measure what happens now. In the first appearance of the structural pattern, the heroic masculine perspective of the opening scene disappeared after the men's exit. Now the resonance persists. Whereas before we could admire Electra's stubborn resistance to the rulers, now, as the revenge plot moves forward, her resolve to act on her own begins to look desperate rather than heroic, an emblem of her exclusion from the *ergon* that the males are pursuing.

The Return of Orestes

The second stasimon (1058–97) rounds out the repeated structural pattern, confirming again the chorus' staunch support of Electra. The song's theme is filial piety, which in the first strophic pair the women find mirrored in the lives of birds. They wish that a "voice that goes beneath the earth" (*chthonia . . . phama*, 1065) would carry a message to the family of Atreus, that the household is sick and the children no longer in accord. Electra is now "betrayed" and tosses alone on the seas, lamenting her father like a nightingale, working to bring down the twin Erinyes who killed him (1058–82). In the remainder of the song, the chorus praises Electra's decision to strive for a "glory bathed in tears." By avenging Agamemnon's murder, she wins the highest prize, observing the greatest laws through piety toward Zeus (1083–97).

The strife between siblings that has isolated Electra would seem to refer to the quarrelling between sisters. But as we have seen, the relationship between Electra and Orestes is also troubled. In the play's early scenes, she complained that he had abandoned her, not answering any of her messages, not returning to help her avenge the murder of Agamemnon. Having overheard the men plotting, we the audience may go further and observe that Orestes's pursuit of revenge puts another kind of distance between brother and sister. As the old slave asserts in the very first scene, Electra's anguished laments—on the basis of which we identify her as hero—cannot be allowed to slow down the pursuit of the revenge. Finally, we remember that Clytemnestra's prayer to Apollo seemed to be answered by the entrance of the god's agent, the Paedagogus. This pattern reappears in the second stasimon, as the women's wish for a "voice that goes beneath the earth" (*chthonia . . . phama*, 1065) to speak to the family of Atreus is followed by the appearance of Orestes in disguise.

Now comes an extraordinary scene.[47] Orestes enters with Pylades and two attendants, carrying an empty urn that supposedly holds the ashes of the dead "Orestes." Once again, the appearance of male avengers is followed by a lengthy lament from Electra (1126–70). Ironies abound as we listen to this outburst of powerful emotion. Now the absence of Orestes, which prompted Electra's first moving monologue, seems to be made final by the presence of his remains. But we—and the avengers—know, as Electra does not, that he is in fact now finally not only present but alive. Orestes has, as he predicted, died "in word" but lives in fact. For Electra, he was only "bright" (*lampron*, 1130) when she sent him away to exile as an infant, but we know that his boast in the prologue is about to be fulfilled:

> Just so, I glory in knowing that from this story
> I shall, alive, shine (*lampsein*) on my enemies like a star.
>
> (59–66)

Electra, meanwhile, who hates deceit, is unwittingly enlisted in the deception of the avengers. Her lament, for all its power, is simply another performance, a *logos*, parallel to the old slave's exciting but false report on the chariot race.[48] Here, as in that earlier context, we see dramatic performance used as a tool for manipulating an audience, hiding the truth in order to achieve the outcome validated by the traditional myth. And because her passionate words are all based on a lie, the emotions behind them are detached from what is real, and thus devalued.[49] When the Paedagogus tells his tale, its truth or falsehood has no bearing on our evaluation of him. As an agent of revenge his job is to fool the royal couple, and he succeeds. Electra's hold on us, by contrast, is founded on her principled refusal to accept what she understands as unjust, the murder of her father and her own subsequent victimization. Once the connection between her emotions and reality is undermined, she loses the basis on which her authenticity as hero has rested.

Earlier, the old slave pulled Orestes away from listening to Electra's first monody, as if exposure to his sister's pain would sap his heroic drive to act. Now that danger would seem to have passed, since she has been drawn into the machinations of the revenge plot. Yet still her emotions have their power over him. In the recognition scene that follows, we will see the pull of Electra's passion working on her brother. As they trade lines back and forth, his glib, can-do self-confidence, so evident in the prologue, recedes in the face of her suffering. Words, which seemed so easy to use because they were attached to nothing real, come harder now:

> Alas, what can I say? Where should I go
> since words fail me? I can no longer control my tongue.

> (1174–75)

When the full weight of her misery becomes clear to him, Orestes is finally pulled into contact with her pain: "I alone have come, feeling pain at your troubles" (1200). Instead of delaying him, as the Paedagogus had feared, her suffering now drives him into action:

ORESTES
Let go of that urn, so you may learn everything.

ELECTRA
By the gods, do not do (*ergasēi*) this to me, stranger!

ORESTES
Be persuaded by my words (*legonti*), and you will not miss the mark.

> (1205–7)

For the next twenty or so lines, the siblings struggle over the urn, as a rapid exchange in iambic trimeters represents their mounting agitation (1210–32). The excitement comes to a crescendo with *antilabē*, the metrical and grammatical units of the verse now divided between the two characters. We have seen a lyric version of this style earlier, between Electra and the chorus. Here, the occasion is a recognition scene, as brother and sister finally reunite. Recognition scenes are at least as old in Greek literature as the *Odyssey*, where Odysseus repeatedly moves from anonymous stranger to glorious hero, making his way homeward across the seas, ending in the great reunion with Penelope in Book 23 of the poem. The dynamics of such a scene offer a rich array of possibilities for the storyteller. A common denominator in all such encounters is high emotion, joy at finding someone who has been lost, fear at the prospect of some delayed reckoning. Sophocles has been building toward this moment at least since the Paedagogus's false tale of the chariot race, where the apparent loss of Orestes crushes Electra. By creating now a concrete symbol of the supposedly dead man, the playwright ratchets up the emotion yet further before Orestes finally releases his sister from her torment.

There are, of course, two layers of theater here.[50] The male avengers have themselves orchestrated Electra's pain in both scenes, manipulating her to forward their plot. Her pain is, we might say, collateral damage for them, a necessary sacrifice for the greater good of revenge. For us, the ebb and flow of emotion created by the layering is complex. Electra's pain in both scenes adds to the joy of the final reunion. Our response to the avengers, meanwhile, might well be a mix of admiration for their cleverness and some distaste for their willingness to use Electra. The precedent of the *Odyssey* surfaces again. Odysseus and Athena do not inform Penelope that her husband has returned, prolonging her pain while benefiting from her resourceful manipulation of the suitors. But Homer's poem consistently valorizes the returning hero's use of deceit, inviting us to admire his cunning. The atmosphere is different in this play, with its ambiguous portrait of Orestes's pride in his own duplicity, colored by the ongoing debates in Athenian society about the nature of human excellence.

Once the recognition is complete, capped by the embrace of the siblings, the exchange modulates into a lyric dialogue, with Electra singing in meters associated with high emotion and Orestes—with two exceptions—answering in iambic trimeters (1232–87). Found elsewhere in several plays of Euripides, this form of exchange emphasizes a different level of emotion in the two speakers, trimeters being the medium for a more measured tone.[51] That distinction would seem to fit here. Electra's joy keeps bubbling up in song, while her brother tries to restrain her for fear of arousing suspicion from the palace: "Better to be silent, lest someone in the palace should hear" (1238). Once again, he invokes *kairos*: "Don't wish to speak at length when it is not the right moment (*kairos*)" (1259).

Sophocles's metrical practice here differs from that of Euripides in that his dialogue is organized into strophe, antistrophe, and epode, with strict metrical corresponsion. On the one hand, the extra degree of formality in Sophocles's style could perhaps heighten the distinction between speakers. But the boundaries break down in the epode: at line 1276 Orestes begins a syncopated form of the trimeter, and at 1280, he speaks in a lyric rhythm at the moment when he affirms her right to express joy without restraint. We should be wary of loading too much significance onto a few syllables, but perhaps the metrical shift suggests that Electra has drawn Orestes further into her world of emotion.[52] Up until the recognition scene, the male avengers have remained aloof from the pull of Electra's pain, content to use her as part of their revenge plot. But now Orestes's defenses have been breached by filial attachment, and he becomes more emotional himself in his response to Electra's passion, both negative and positive.[53]

The old slave's entrance at line 1326 would seem to confirm this interpretation. He is appalled at the siblings' lack of self-control:

You utter and witless fools!
Do you no longer care about your lives?
Have you no innate sense?
Do you not see that you are not just near
but right in the middle of the greatest dangers?

(1326–30)

Electra seemed to have been safely under control, part of the males' plot. Now the tide has reversed and Orestes has succumbed to the dangerous pull of feminine emotion from which the Paedagogus managed to drag him away at the end of the prologue. Luckily, says the old slave, he has been on guard at the doors to the palace, or they would have been caught already. But they must now "get free of your long speeches (*makrōn logōn*) and insatiate shouts of joy"; delay is dangerous and now is the "right moment" (*akmē*) to wind things up (1335–38).

Orestes is brought around by this warning. He asks how things stand in the palace, and the Paedagogus keeps the pressure up: "I'll let you know when the plot is coming to fruition" (1344). But then Electra breaks into the plotting again, asking who the old slave is. After some coy hints, Orestes identifies him, and Electra bursts forth again joyfully, "Oh dearest light, only savior of the house of Agamemnon . . ." (1354). She starts to launch yet another recognition scene, going on for another nine lines of ecstatic welcome. The Paedagogus is not moved: "That seems to me to be enough" (1364). There will be plenty of time later for stories (*logous*) about what has happened since she saw him. "Now is the right time to act" (*kairos . . . erdein*, 1368). Orestes gets things back on track, addressing Pylades for the only time in the play:

Let's have no more long speeches (*makrōn . . . logōn*), Pylades;
here is our work; we must go inside right now, once we have
saluted the seats of my father's gods,
who all live in this portico.

(1372–75)

Orestes, Pylades, and the old slave now enter the palace to carry out the first murder. Electra remains onstage for a short prayer to Apollo, asking for the god's help in the punishing of the royal couple's impiety, then follows the others inside (1376–83).

As the revenge plot nears its climax, Electra's isolation appears finally to be at an end. The long arc of Sophocles's story, which began with her completely separated from the men she loved and depended on, alone and in despair, has come to rest here as she walks into the palace to join Orestes. The tonality of this moment, as so often in the play, is mixed. No longer alone, Electra can look forward to a better life, free of abuse from the king and queen. She has survived and may yet prosper. At the same time, we note that this melding with the plotters is the last instance in a series of encounters she has had with them, each one undermining further the heroic authority she carried as a result of her stubborn holdout against the usurping couple. There is, we might say, a dissonance between her mythic status and the emerging reality of her situation in a society ruled by men and their imperatives. This disjunction lies at the heart of Sophocles's dramatic aims in the play.[54]

Vengeance Achieved

The chorus now sings its third song, two strophes hailing the plotters as "inescapable hounds" of vengeance and Orestes as "the cunning champion of the dead." Hermes himself, they say, leads him to his goal, "hiding the plot (*dolos*) in darkness" (1384–97). These last words have caused trouble for those who would like to see the play as an uncomplicated revenge story with a "happy" ending.[55] The "bright" (*lampros*) returning son heading into the dark palace like Hermes to the underworld is not a cheerful tableau. Its tonality will linger, settling over the play's final action, with Orestes shoving Aegisthus into the palace to his death. The next forty-five lines or so are in the form of a conversation, organized in strophic form, between Electra (who returns to the stage after the choral ode), Orestes (who comes back onstage with Pylades in the middle of this dialogue at line 1424), and the chorus, with two vivid interjections by Clytemnestra offstage. The actors usually speak in iambic trimeters, with the chorus weaving in lyric meters. The exception is line 1404, when Clytemnestra is heard crying out in a lyric rhythm associated with high emotion.

Sophocles has Clytemnestra's murder precede that of Aegisthus, reversing the order in both Aeschylus's and Euripides's versions. The usual understanding of this change is that it diminishes the prominence of Clytemnestra's death, which is now only the penultimate murder.[56] Perhaps, but in fact Sophocles focuses more on Clytemnestra's actual death than either of his fellow playwrights.[57] She dies silently offstage in Aeschylus's version; in Euripides's *Electra* we hear her speak once before dying. Here she cries out five times over the course of her murder (1405–16), each time provoking responses from Electra and the chorus. The result is a scene of prolonged intensity, expressed in an elaborately orchestrated strophic style. (One thinks of the storm scene in *Rigoletto.*) She dies in the strophe (1417), and her absence is emphasized by the fact that the verses that would correspond to hers are dropped from the antistrophe, a rare case of imperfect metrical corresponsion. Electra's return to the stage after the choral ode (1398), rather than with Orestes and Pylades following the murder (1424), allows Sophocles to have her reflect on the event as it happens, adding yet more emotional force to the passage. She remains the emotional barometer for the play's action.

No sooner are the conspirators reunited onstage than the chorus spies Aegisthus in the distance, coming toward the palace. The men quickly exit, leaving Electra in charge for the first time: "Leave things here to me" (1436). The ensuing exchange between Aegisthus and Electra is riddled with the irony characteristic of this part of the traditional story, the king glorying in his triumph, Electra pretending to acquiesce while speaking in ironic double entendres. The central doors of the palace open, showing Orestes and Pylades standing beside a bier with Clytemnestra's corpse covered by a shroud. There follows yet another recognition scene, the second time that Orestes has revealed what purport to be the remains of "Orestes." This time fear is the dominant emotion, as Aegisthus uncovers the face and realizes he is doomed:

> Alas, I understand your words; for this must be
> Orestes who speaks to me.

> (1479–80)

Now *logos*, *ergon*, and *kerdos* make a final appearance. Aegisthus asks to say one final word. Electra's blunt response is telling:

> Don't let him say anything more, brother;
> by the gods, do not allow a long speech (*logous*).
> For what profit (*kerdos*) comes from the time
> to a man whose death is delayed, when men are mingled in ruin?
> No! Kill him as quickly as possible, and then throw
> him out to those for whom it is proper to give him burial,
> out of our sight. For only thus will there be
> any release for me from ancient evils.
>
> (1487–90)

Orestes picks up the theme:

> Go inside right now! This is a dispute
> not about words (*logōn*), but about your life.
>
> (1491–92)

The word for "life" here, *psuchēs*, holds the place of *ergon*, the "real" thing to which mere words are contrasted.[58]

Aegisthus does not want to enter the palace. If this is an honorable act, why must it take place in darkness? Why not kill him now, out in the open? Orestes orders him in harshly, the doors close, and the chorus closes the play:

> Oh seed of Atreus, after suffering
> many evils, you have finally come through
> in freedom, finished in this day's struggle.
>
> (1508–10)

The coda is suspect to many scholars, on the grounds of style and content.[59] But since the choral endings of Greek tragedies are not usually memorable, their impact would not be crucial in any event.

The portrait of Electra in this final section of the play, from the first entrance into the palace by the male avengers to the end, has seemed especially harsh to some observers.[60] Her bitter responses to Clytemnestra's outcries, her insistence on a swift death for Aegisthus, her wish that his corpse be left out for scavengers, all seem to be colored by intense hatred. But why would we expect anything else? She sees both Clytemnestra and Aegisthus as irredeemably evil villains who have imprisoned and abused her. An Electra who was suddenly not as bitter and vengeful would be inconsistent with the character we have seen onstage. Her impatience with words that delay the requisite acts certifies that she has finally been assimilated to the perspective of Orestes and the male plotters. At the same time, Orestes's identification with Hermes suggests that he has been pulled toward the dark, chthonic world of Electra. These last scenes bring the royal children into a kind of harmony at last. Whether we should rejoice on Electra's behalf is another question.

Justice Achieved?

Exiting grimly into the palace, Orestes leaves much uncertainty behind. Are we to imagine that the Erinyes hover offstage, waiting to pursue Orestes as they do in Aeschylus and Euripides? Did Sophocles, the most Homeric of playwrights, mean to present an uncomplicated revenge story, modeled on the version in the *Odyssey*? Among scholars no definitive consensus has emerged.[61] The variety of opinions is understandable, since Sophocles declines to settle things. Aeschylus escaped the moral conflict inherent in private, retaliatory justice by not advocating for one side or the other within the royal family, but by expanding the venue for justice to include a third party, the *polis*. Euripides recasts the conflict in the open air of the countryside, another kind of expansion. Sophocles, in contrast to both, seems intent on narrowing the focus to the airless atmosphere of the palace. Orestes's insistence on forcing Aegisthus into the dark is a microcosmic version of the entire play. Once he has closed off the exits, Sophocles complicates things further, as we have seen, by creating deeper, more rounded characters than Aeschylus. Relatively abstract concepts like "justice" are hard to pin down within the rich and often contradictory dynamic between the principal characters.

No greater clarity comes from looking to the gods for guidance: as so often in Sophoclean drama, they are powerful, influential, and opaque. Artemis, so the myth goes (and Electra reminds us), demanded retribution for Agamemnon killing a deer in her sacred precinct. For this death Clytemnestra exacts retribution. Apollo, meanwhile, through his oracle has ordered Orestes to avenge his father's murder. No intervention from Athena decides, as in Aeschylus, which of her fellow deities is on the right side of justice. The Erinyes, the traditional agents of vengeance against those who murder someone related by blood, do not appear at the end of the play to hound Orestes for his matricide, as they do in the Aeschylean and Euripdean versions. There is, however, no shortage of references to the Erinyes elsewhere in the play. Electra prays to the Erinyes to avenge her father's murder in her first monologue (112), and is identified with them by the chorus, as one of the "inescapable hounds of vengeance" (1386–87). The chorus summons the Erinyes, along with "Justice" (*Dika*, 476), to help Electra (491), but then hails Electra as the one who would bring down the "Twin Erinyes," Clytemnestra and Aegisthus (1080). These earth deities will not, it appears, provide any more guidance than the Olympians.

The end of the play is certainly dark. Those inclining to a pessimistic view of Orestes's prospects point to this pervasive tonality. That he is compared to Hermes the guide of souls in his final act makes sense in that Aegisthus is clearly headed for Hades, but it may also suggest that he himself is moving into a dark future. In itself, this conclusion might seem to tip the scales against an uncomplicated triumph for the avengers. Perhaps Sophocles wanted to question, however subtly, the confidence that Agamemnon's children have in the rightness of their revenge. But beyond these few hints, none of them in my view definitive, Sophocles supplies little to help us decide if "justice" has been done, or even what that term might mean in the context of this work.

Because we are used to looking at this play through the lens of earlier versions of the myth, Homeric and Aeschylean (and perhaps Euripidean), we persist in thinking that Sophocles must have aimed to provide an analogously settled view of the moral tangles inherent in the revenge story. But given the absence of any decisive arguments one way or the other, we might try approaching the play from another direction. Rather than searching for ever more subtle clues as to how the playwright might have intended us to view the outcome of the drama in the context of the traditional myth, perhaps we should follow Sophocles's lead: maybe we are asking the play for answers it was not intended to provide.[62]

Form and Meaning

Our discussion so far has emphasized elements in the drama that seem to create a certain detachment from the traditional myth and its inherent motivations. First, there is the separation of the play's designated hero from the action of the revenge story. As we have seen, the plot to murder Clytemnestra and Aegisthus is launched by Orestes and his henchmen without Electra's knowledge or, initially, participation. Electra's credentials as Sophoclean hero are established only after the men have left the stage, expressed verbally through her refusal to bend to the will of the rulers. She assumes this stance, articulated through a series of encounters with other women, in the chorus and in her family, in complete ignorance of the avengers' plans. By segregating the female characters from the men and their plotting, Sophocles harmonizes two polarities, male/female and action/emotion. For the first 660 lines men are portrayed as actors, women as reactors. This division mirrors, in some respects, the Greeks' beliefs about the nature of men and women. But Sophocles creates ironic crosscurrents of meaning by further refracting these disjunctions through the polarity *logos/ergon*, the site of vigorous fifth century debate about, among other things, human nature. Orestes exults in his ability to die in words but triumph in deeds; Electra scorns her sister's refusal to bring her words into harmony with her actions; she sees herself, meanwhile, as acting against the rulers through her words, but also looks to Orestes to bring her words of defiance to fruition through his own actions.

The segregation of men and women onstage ends with the entrance of the Paedagogus, bringing to Clytemnestra the false story of Orestes's death. The old slave's return also marks the start of a repetition, which we noted above, of the pattern of scenes from lines 1–515. As we said there, in the second iteration of the sequence Electra's authority as hero is undermined. As we watch her respond to the false death of her brother, the outpouring of emotion, which previously was a reflection of her principled refusal to condone the actual murder of Agamemnon, now becomes an index of her exclusion from the action of the revenge plot. Her words remain powerful. But unmoored from reality, the emotion becomes ironic, denatured. We can almost imagine the old slave stifling a smile. Sophoclean heroes can weather many kinds of failure, but being the object of laughter is deadly. When Athena invites Odysseus to laugh at the maddened Ajax in the opening scene of his play, we know the great warrior is in deep trouble.[63]

The parallel with Ajax is apt here, since in both cases we are invited, along with some of the actors onstage, to view a piece of theater generated by deceit. Athena makes Ajax think he has murdered the leaders of the Greek expedition at Troy in retaliation for denying him the arms of the fallen Achilles. We know that he has slaughtered cattle, and we see him covered in their gore. The old slave convinces Clytemnestra and Electra that Orestes has died in a chariot race, prompting a passionate and prolonged expression of pain from the latter. We know he has only died "in word," and so Electra's pain, like Ajax's exultation, is the product not of heroic strength but delusion. The irony returns in an even stronger form when Orestes allows Electra to hold the urn and pour out an anguished eulogy to her "dead" brother.

Because Orestes's distress at witnessing Electra's eulogy leads him to break the barrier of deception between himself and his sister, Electra's exclusion from the revenge plot ends (1174ff.). The ironies generated by her ignorance fade and we begin to see that her leverage onstage rises again somewhat as Orestes is momentarily pulled in by her emotions, just as the Paedagogus feared. The old slave reasserts discipline and the plot moves forward to its dark conclusion. The recognition scene between siblings comes later than one might expect, delayed by the first of two false recognitions of a "dead" Orestes, the urn scene and the unveiling of Clytemnestra's corpse for Aegisthus. By manipulating this conventional element of the revenge story, Sophocles calls attention to its artificiality and—again—prompts some detachment by the audience from the myth's urgencies.

Ironic detachment of the sort prompted by Sophocles's dramaturgy in this play is something rather more common to comic than tragic narrative in Greek literature. Encountering a tragic story, whether in a text or in the theater, usually puts before us a world in which words and deeds are presented as irrevocable. "Once blood is spilled, who can call it back?" says the chorus of *Agamemnon* (1018–21). The fact of mortality represents the most universal and irrevocable aspect of human experience as viewed from the tragic perspective. Comic narrative, by contrast, tends to have as its goal the restoration of order. No matter how disturbed things become, comic stories depend on our belief that they can be put right again. The *Odyssey*, our first comic narrative, establishes from the outset that Odysseus can and must be restored to his prior status as king, husband, father, and son. His restoration in turn will guarantee the return of right order in Ithaka.

Deceit is acceptable in the comic narrative if it is in the service of restoration. Plautus's comic slave can lie and manipulate others with impunity, as long as he arranges for the rich man's son to be reunited with his girlfriend. Disguise, a special form of deceit, is particularly useful in comic stories because it allows for characters to assume temporarily a new identity in pursuit of their goals. The false persona is fine in the service of restoration and as long as it can be put aside. Odysseus's disguise as beggar in the royal palace is not seen as dishonorable, only efficacious. In tragic narratives, on the other hand, deceit of any kind is suspect, a sign of bad character and unworthy motives. Odysseus is a different character in the *Iliad* than the *Odyssey*. He is admired in the former for his speaking ability, but his penchant for lying is not a part of his persona. Achilles, as we have seen, hates people who say one thing and believe another.

The hero of a story, whose perspective tends to guide our own, reflects the narrative form. The tragic hero is passionately engaged with the world, open to people and things in it. S/he is so in part because the stakes are high: no going back. Comic heroes, by contrast, must remain emotionally detached from the world and its people, so as to be able to effect the proper outcome. Artifice, the badge of excellence in a comic hero, needs detachment, which aids manipulation. Authenticity is not a desirable trait in a comic hero. If you need to change your identity to achieve the desired outcome, existential angst is inconvenient.

The description of a comic hero sketched above fits Orestes, as he appears in the prologue, pretty snugly. Happy to lie and manipulate others as long as he can win glory, he approaches the murder of his own mother with self-confident insouciance. Effecting the proper outcome is paramount for him, regardless of the cost to others. Electra is the polar opposite of this persona, passionately engaged with others, either hating or loving them, she is scornfully dismissive of her sister's attempts to avoid conflict.[64] Everything that has happened is, in the world created by her powerful emotions, beyond remedy—her miserable, childless condition, the disgraceful behavior of her mother. Time is measured out in endless repetition of suffering, from which she sees no escape. Only Orestes can break this cycle for her, acting from outside it.

Conclusion: An Inconvenient Hero

In Electra Sophocles creates one of his most powerful and most disturbing heroes. Like Homer's Achilles, she maintains a steady pitch of high emotion as events swirl around her. Onstage for almost the entire play, she dominates our attention, though within the story her own fortunes rise and fall with circumstances. Forbiddingly austere, she is isolated by her suffering. Though Orestes can at first assume something akin to the trickster persona, confident in his ability to control and manipulate others to achieve his ends, Electra can only play the role of his passionate dupe.[65] Because she is so compelling, we can be confident that Sophocles means for the form of his play to be experienced as challenging in the context of traditional retellings of the myth. To return to our earlier question, what can "justice" mean to such a character? Indeed, would there ever be any salvation for the woman we see created onstage?

These questions prompt further thought about Sophocles's insistence on segregating his hero from the action of the revenge plot. The traditional story, as we find it in the earlier versions of Homer and Aeschylus, supplies motivations for the principal characters. Orestes and Electra can be healed eventually by the deaths of Clytemnestra and Aegisthus; the heroic determination of the returning son, supported by his adoring sister, finally effects justice for the family. Sophocles's play begins with the confident assertions of Orestes, but once Electra enters, the solidarity of the siblings breaks down. Electra's passionate emotions, the foundation of her portrait as hero, are seen by the male avengers as threatening the successful completion of their mission. So when Orestes recognizes his sister and begins to be pulled into the dark swirl of her emotions, his focus on the action required by the plot fades and the old slave must pull him back on track. From the perspective of the revenge plot, Electra's pain is irrelevant to the achieving of justice, except insofar as it fuels her performance as grieving sister, which can be used by the plotters to deceive the royal couple. To put it the other way around, Orestes's briskly efficient pursuit of revenge cannot survive a confrontation with the genuine emotional damage resulting from the events of the family history, including his own recent actions. The old story will not provide a satisfying answer to the problems embodied by Electra.

Not only does the old story come under scrutiny but also the medium through which it is told. Athenian tragic drama, a central feature of annual religious festivals, had served for a century as a vehicle for the display of communal pride and the addressing of communal fears. Now Sophocles would appear to be calling the art form itself into question as a reliable mirror of the city's fundamental values. The false recognition scenes occasioned by the avengers' plot and Electra's searing performance with the urn show instead the potential in dramatic performance for deceiving and manipulating its audience.

Sophocles, nearing the end of his long and illustrious career as a citizen, soldier, and artist, must have looked on the current state of Athens with dismay. Depleted by the war, its faith in the democratic political system shaken, the city faced an uncertain future at best. It would not be surprising then to see the playwright reevaluating both the traditional stories he and others had turned to for guidance and the art form he had perfected to express them.[66] In his last two plays, we will see this exploration continue, accompanied by a reimagining of the central heroic figure he had done so much to establish in his earlier plays.

CHAPTER 3

Philoctetes

The Creature in the Cave

He is the one the god said to bring.

(Sophocles, *Philoctetes*, 840)

Philoctetes opens, like *Electra*, with two men plotting. That one of them is Odysseus would have signaled to an audience in 409 BCE that deception is likely afoot. By the late fifth century, Homer's hero had become the paradigm for the clever, shifty speaker who manipulates others with words.[1] His opening lines set the scene for the play: "This is the shore of the seagirt island of Lemnos,/ neither trod upon nor lived in by humans" (1–2). It is hard to imagine a venue more different from the stifling atmosphere of the royal place in *Electra*. The central doors of the *skene* now will be the mouth of a cave on a deserted island. And while the previous play features long stretches with only women onstage, dominated by an angry princess, this story will have all male characters.[2]

If the flavor of *Electra*'s opening scene, with its epic compound adjectives and aristocratic masculine perspective, was decidedly heroic, here the tone is more like what we would now call anthropological.[3] Odysseus orders his companion Neoptolemus to search out a cave with two mouths—which he presumably remembers from when he left Philoctetes there on the way to Troy ten years before—admitting sun in the winter, cool breezes in the summer. Near it will be a spring. Neoptolemus finds the cave immediately (presumably the *skēnē* had a back door):[4]

NEOPTOLEMUS
I see an empty dwelling, with no man.

ODYSSEUS
Are there things needed for making a home inside?

NEOPTOLEMUS
Yes, trampled-down leaves as if for someone living there.

ODYSSEUS
The rest is empty, with nothing under the roof?

NEOPTOLEMUS
There's a cup, made from one piece of wood, the work
of a bad craftsman, and stones for making a fire.

ODYSSEUS
Those treasures you mention must be his.

NEOPTOLEMUS
Aha! Here's something else: rags being
dried by the sun, stained with pus from some sore.

(31–39)

Odysseus anxiously calls for a scout to keep watch lest Philoctetes return and surprise them. He cannot have gotten far on a bad foot and would like nothing better than to attack Odysseus. Sophocles introduces here a central theme in the play. *Where* Philoctetes is will be crucial for his role as hero.

The island venue, the cave with its curious furnishings, the absent dweller whose return is an occasion for fear, all this would remind the audience of nothing so much as the Cyclops episode from the *Odyssey*.[5] Like Polyphemus, Philoctetes is physically repellant and nurses a powerful anger against Odysseus; isolated on an uncivilized island, he falls prey to the wily hero and his companions. Seen through the eyes of his relentless pursuer, Philoctetes becomes a kind of monster here, whose howling and screaming drove away the Greeks (11), whose crude lair is an anthropological curiosity.[6] In *Electra*, Sophocles narrows down the scope of the story to an intense crucible of hatred and deception. Now he opens up the lens to include all of the earth's creatures, human and animal, savage and civilized, specimens exposed on an empty island.[7] In the *Odyssey*, the Cyclops episode prompts meditation on the Golden Age myth and its implications for the nature of human civilization in the larger context of the cosmos. By invoking the mythical paradigm here, Sophocles perhaps hints at a quandary to come: who will be the savage in this play, who the civilizing hero?[8]

The Battle for Neoptolemus

With the area secured, Odysseus returns to plotting. The goal is to capture the bow of Herakles, which Philoctetes now has.[9] Without it, Troy cannot fall to the Greeks. As the man who betrayed Philoctetes before, Odysseus cannot let himself be seen while the latter has the bow or he will die and take Neoptolemus down with him. The challenge for him will be to convince the son of the famously straightforward Achilles to win over Philoctetes with lies. The anthropological cast of the previous lines is now modulated to reappear in the familiar terms of fifth-century Athenian intellectual life.[10] Neoptolemus must not only be noble (*gennaion*)[11] with his body (*sōmati*) but ready to try something new:

> You must ensnare the soul
> of Philoctetes with your words (*logoisi*).
> When he asks you who you are and where
> you are from, say "the son of Achilles;" no need to lie.
> Say you are sailing home, leaving the fleet
> of the Achaeans, filled up with hatred of them
> who fetched you from home, begging,
> as their only hope of taking Ilium.

> (54–61)

The hard sell follows shortly:

> ODYSSEUS
> I know, my son, that by nature (*phusei*) you are not the kind of man
> to say such words or plot harm against others.
> But it is sweet to win the prize of victory,

so take courage; in time we will be shown just.
Now give yourself to me for a brief time,
and after that you will be renowned as the most dutiful of mortals.

(79–85)

The son of Achilles is predictably reluctant:

NEOPTOLEMUS
Son of Laertes, those things it pains me to hear,
such things I also hate to do.
It is not my nature (*ephun*) to work through evil treachery,
neither mine nor that of him who begot (*ekphusas*) me.

(86–89)

Neoptolemus will use force but not trickery. After all, how could a man with one good foot get the better of them? He would rather fail acting honorably than win through evil means. Odysseus now takes the role of wise mentor:

Son of an excellent father, I too was young once,
with a quiet tongue and an active hand.
But now I see that put to trial the tongue,
not actions, rules in all things for mortals.[12]

(96–99)

Parallels with the prologue of *Electra* begin to surface. Odysseus takes the lead in plotting with his younger charge as does the Paedagogus with Orestes. There is no time for lengthy speeches (*akmē . . . ou makrōn hēmin logōn*, 12; cf. *El.* 22); they must proceed quietly (*sīga*, 22); once again the polarity of *logos/ergon* informs the dialogue, with *sōma*, "body," the instrument for action, holding the place of *ergon* (51).[13] But the duality plays a different—and larger—role in this exchange: whereas Orestes throws in an offhand reference to dying in word but not in fact, Odysseus builds his case firmly on the opposition. Because it is the mentor who is identified with suspect sophistic rhetoric here, not his pupil as is the case in *Electra*, and the mentor is a famous hero, not a servant—however revered—claims made for the new rhetoric carry more weight.

But genealogy complicates the power balance. However convincing a speaker Odysseus is, Neoptolemus carries the aura of his powerful father, giving him a moral weight not usually associated with younger men. As he says, it is not his "inborn nature" (*phusis*) to use deception. The Greek word is regularly opposed to *nomos*, "custom," in fifth-century Athens, a polarity analogous to *logos/ergon* in its conjuring of the ongoing negotiations over the source of human excellence.[14] Indeed, the first half of the play might well be understood on one level as a battle for the soul of Neoptolemus, with the victory as a referendum on the differing moral perspectives—and their afterlife in Athenian culture—of Homer's most famous heroes.[15] Will the young man adopt the slippery, sophistic ethics of Odysseus, letting a desire for victory justify deception, or will he embody Achilles's old-fashioned insistence that actions be consistent with words? Sophocles points here to a burning issue in the intellectual debates of the time: can virtue (*aretē*) be taught, or must it be part of one's genetic inheritance?[16] The verdict will not be rendered until late in the play.

Neoptolemus is not quite ready to commit himself. The ensuing exchange further refines the vocabulary of deception. In a rapid exchange, Odysseus defends the use of trickery (*dolōi*, 101) and lying, if the result is profit (*kerdos*, 111; cf. *El.* 61).[17] He is certain that Philoctetes cannot be persuaded (*peisant'*, 102) nor taken by force (*bian*, 103). Neoptolemus remains skeptical: Is Odysseus urging him simply to tell lies (*pseudē*, 100)? Is it not disgraceful (*aischron*, 107) to do so? Finally, after Odysseus dangles yet more inducements, the chance to ensure Troy's capture, a reputation for wisdom (*sophos*) and valor (*agathos*), Neoptolemus yields: "So be it! I will do it, casting aside all shame" (120). Odysseus outlines the plan: Neoptolemus must wait for Philoctetes, while Odysseus hides. He will send a sailor from the ship with some story or other, and Neoptolemus must gain some advantage from the words (*sumpheronta tōn aei logōn*, 131).

Though Neoptolemus yields for the moment to his older companion, the tension between the two views of ethical conduct injected here by the Homeric allusions will run through the entire play. There is no corresponding tension between the plotters in *Electra*. Orestes, though identified in the prologue with an aristocratic perspective, is entirely on board with the use of deception his servant promotes. The counterweight in that play to the shifty behavior of the plotters is Electra. As we will see, Philoctetes plays a similar role.

Parodos: Plotting and Pity

Odysseus exits along with the silent scout, leaving Neoptolemus on stage for the first entrance of the chorus made up of the young man's sailors.[18] In the versions of the story produced by Aeschylus and Euripides, now mostly lost to us, Lemnians formed the chorus.[19] Sophocles's innovation further isolates Philoctetes and reinforces the sense of him as living in the margins of nature and culture, a liminal existence prompting curiosity—soon to be voiced by the chorus—about the effects of his enforced solitude. As the sailors make clear immediately, their allegiance is to Neoptolemus alone. At the same time, while participating fully in the deception of Philoctetes, these men will also occasionally display sympathy for the disabled exile, increasing our distaste for Odysseus's manipulation of him and mirroring the ambivalence of Neoptolemus.[20]

The form of the parodos repeats Sophocles's innovation in the entrance song of the chorus of *Electra*. Here as there, the chorus shares its first song with an actor. Neoptolemus's contributions are predominantly in anapests, whereas Electra, after her initial monody in anapests, echoes the chorus' lyric meters, but the mingling of voices in both cases integrates the chorus into the action more smoothly and complicates the perspective of the parodos.[21]

The sailors begin by declaring their allegiance to Neoptolemus: they are willing to do their part to deceive Philoctetes. What should they, strangers in a strange land, hide and what reveal to the suspicious outcast? Skill and judgment reside with the man who wields the scepter of Zeus and they await his orders (135–43). The sailors' dependence on their captain is reminiscent of the chorus of *Ajax*, in awe of their master, ready to do whatever he wants (*Ajax* 134–71). These sailors defer to their young master's "ancient power" (*kratos ōgugion*, 142), reminding him (and us) that Neoptolemus is the son of Achilles, whose regal force they see in his son. Conjuring implicitly both Ajax and Achilles, the chorus reinforces the contrast to Odysseus, the other model for adult manhood available at the moment.

In reply, Neoptolemus invites them to inspect the lair of the absent "awesome traveler." When the latter returns, they should help however they can by following their leader's hand signals (144–49). The chorus again affirms its readiness to work for his advantage (*kairōi*, 151) and follow his lead, then return to the intriguing topic of the stranger's habitat. The sailors need to know all they can, lest Philoctetes get the drop on them. What kind of dwelling does he have, on what land? Where does he rest? Is he close by or distant (150–58)? Neoptolemus points out the cave with two mouths but is interrupted by another anxious question: where has he gone? He is off looking for food, shooting birds with his bow, painfully in his pain, having no one to heal his wounds (159–68).

The chorus now turns from detached curiosity to compassion. They pity this wretched man, always alone, suffering from his savage sickness, wandering at a loss as he encounters each arising need. Oh unhappy race of mortals, for whom there is no tolerable existence! This man may be of noble stock, but he is alone in life, bereft and living among shaggy beasts, with no one to hear his bitter cries. Neoptolemus fills in the back story of Philoctetes's wound from the snake bite at the altar of Chryse, apparently the work of the gods, who wanted him kept out of action until the time arrived for him to bring down Troy with his bow (169–200).

The exchange so far has reinforced the portrait of Philoctetes as an object of fascination: abandoned on the empty island, scratching out a miserable existence with no one to heal his wound. To this detached, anthropological perspective are juxtaposed two emotions that suggest a closer engagement: fear of the cave dweller and compassion for his plight. Analogies with Polyphemus persist and focus our attention on the awesome loner.[22] And once again, the question of where Philoctetes is comes to the forefront.

The Dreaded Traveler Returns

The sailors shush their captain. They have heard a noise from offstage. The sound might well be from a man laboring under some constraint, the anguished cry of one who struggles. Better take care: he's very close now. The sound he makes is not like the music from the pipes of a shepherd living in the wild. No, it sounds as if he's stumbling along, shouting. His cry is frightening (211–18). Like Electra, Philoctetes is heard before he is seen and the sounds he makes cause both curiosity and wariness.[23] The Paedagogus has to guard against Orestes being distracted from the job at hand by Electra's pain; here the plotters' caution reflects the Polyphemus paradigm: some strange, semi-human creature might be approaching.[24]

Philoctetes's first words echo Homer's monster:

> Hail, strangers!
> Who are you, who have put in to this deserted land
> that lacks a good harbor?
>
> (219–21)

> Oh strangers, who are you? What watery path have you sailed?
> Are you wandering on some reckless errand like
> pirates on the sea, who risk their lives bringing evil to strangers?
>
> (*Od.* 9, 252–54)

In the exchange that follows, Sophocles presents his "monster" in an entirely sympathetic light, playing against the implications of the Polyphemus paradigm. Not only does he greet his visitors warmly—the Greek language is the "most beloved of sounds" (234); when Neoptolemus identifies himself, he is "child of the dearest father," from a "dear land" (242)—but his joy at discovering that he is in the presence of Greeks also establishes his credentials as a civilized man immediately, for his visitors and for an Athenian audience.[25] Recognition of his part in the Trojan expedition supplies a larger, heroic context within human civilization for his present distress: he is not a nameless, pathetic victim but the son of a famous man, a wounded warrior. In this wider context, the account he gives of his terrible treatment at the hands of the Greek commanders not only produces sympathy from Neoptolemus but also perhaps rehabilitates somewhat his claims to masculine authority. Addressing the young man before him, he uses the words *teknon* (236, 260, 276, 300, 307) and *pais* (242, 260, 315, 327), terms inviting some level of intimacy ("my boy"; "my child") but also signaling his status as the young man's elder. Odysseus uses both words continually while working on the sensibilities of his intended protégé. Philoctetes, we now see, will be yet a third possible mentor for Neoptolemus.[26]

Neoptolemus's questions about his part in the Trojan expedition prompt a long catalog of miseries from the stranded warrior (254–316). Philoctetes's speech shares many themes with Electra's lengthy lament to the chorus after her initial monody (*El.* 254–309). Both heroes resent bitterly their isolation, their betrayal and abandonment by those who should support them; for both time passes slowly, in repeated cycles of unending suffering. The similarities in tone and circumstance might seem surprising in two plays so apparently different in other respects. But we will see that Philoctetes recalls the bitter princess in many ways.[27] His wound imposes physical restrictions on him that mirror Electra's confinement in the palace.[28] Her wound is emotional, his physical, but the consequent suffering, expressed in noisy complaints, causes each to be shunned. Both are dressed in rags and physically repellent, both fall prey in their powerlessness to the manipulation of unscrupulous travelers, both will serve as embodiments of an inconvenient preference for principled integrity over situational ethics.

Even the gender difference between the plotters and their unwitting victim in *Electra* reappears in *Philoctetes*. Though *Philoctetes* is unique among extant Sophoclean plays for its all-male cast of characters, its hero is feminized by his wound and his abandonment. Unable to fight, lacking any opponents beyond the birds he hunts with his bow, he cannot exert himself to win the *kleos* that signifies masculine heroic status.[29] His wound oozes; women were thought by the Greeks to "leak," thus bringing the danger of pollution.[30] The Greek army was repelled by the bad smell of his foot; the Greek myth of the "Lemnian women" has them abandoned on the island because they smell bad.[31] Philoctetes's relationship to time also mirrors Electra's. Like her, he experiences time as measured by the rhythms of nature, whereas the preoccupation with timing, *kairos* and *akmē*, so prominent in the plotting of the Paedagogus and Orestes, is confined, as we have seen, to the machinations of Odysseus and his allies.

Sophocles has shaped our perception of his characters so as to set up a rich and evolving interplay of perspectives. Our attention focuses first on Odysseus and Neoptolemus, the older man working to win the younger's allegiance. As the scene unfolds, that struggle is filtered through Homeric paradigms of ethical conduct, which in turn reflect contemporary intellectual and political issues arising from the impact of democratic reforms in Athens. Next, the chorus is added to the mix, recruited to support Odysseus's plan to deceive Philoctetes. They are willing but also voicesome compassion for the wounded man, foreshadowing Neoptolemus's eventual ambivalence toward his commander's plan and thus keeping the original contest for the young man's soul present in our minds. Philoctetes we see at first only through the eyes of the newly arrived travelers. Parallels with Homer's Polyphemus underscore the wounded man's liminal position, living as a kind of diminished creature beyond the pale of human civilization, and raise the possibility that he will be similarly hostile and frightening. Until he actually appears on stage and speaks, we—and the other characters—see Philoctetes from a detached perspective that precludes any real understanding of him as a person.

Once he does appear, his exchanges with the chorus and Neoptolemus alter our perception by making him emotionally accessible as a human being. At the same time, his elevated status, from an uncivilized, semi-human outcast to a potentially empowered Greek male, raises the question of his relationship to the heroic mission of Odysseus and Neoptolemus. Like Orestes and the Paedagogus, these two men arrive onstage to do the work of the traditional myth. They must succeed or Troy cannot fall. As in *Electra*, they encounter an immobile figure who must be manipulated for them to reach their goal. In both cases, the indirect connection of this figure to the heroic action of the plot creates a tension in the play, which Sophocles exploits to alter our perspective on the traditional story.

In *Philoctetes*, we see Sophocles continuing the experiment he began with *Electra* but altering the dynamic between his hero and the myth. An Athenian audience might well expect Orestes to be the hero of *Electra*, as he is in the versions of Homer and Aeschylus. By instead deflecting our attention onto Electra, the playwright urges us to widen our understanding of how the heroic action of the myth affects those who are not its direct agents. The early scenes of *Philoctetes*, where Philoctetes is relegated to the role of a repellant curiosity, might seem to present Neoptolemus as the potential hero of the play. But once the wounded exile begins to command our attention as a person in his own right, his connection to the heroic mission of the travelers draws our attention. Unlike Electra, who must be co-opted into the plot so as not to impede its completion, Philoctetes is the central figure in the mythical story, upon whose location at Troy the entire heroic mission eventually depends. The relationship between Electra's desires and the will of the gods is never clarified; Philoctetes, though not an active agent of divine will, is the most important vehicle for its fulfillment.

Deception, Stage 1: Parade of Heroes

Neoptolemus now begins the long process of persuading Philoctetes to give him the bow. Odysseus has provided him with a handy set of lies with which to get the job done (58–69): he is to tell Philoctetes that the Greek commanders begged him to come to Troy, since otherwise the city would not fall; that when he arrived at Sigeum, they revealed that they had already given his father's weapons to Odysseus; that he, being angry at the commanders, sailed away for home (343–90).[32] Odysseus has suggested earlier not only that the bow was necessary for Troy to fall but that Neoptolemus himself could take the city with the famous weapon (113–15). Whether this last prospect will turn out to be true remains to be seen. For now, it becomes part of Neoptolemus's own deceptive speech (345–47).

The shabby treatment the young man describes at the hands of the Greek commanders is meant to foster sympathy and fellow-feeling from Philoctetes. From our perspective, the speech is full of ironies. In order to dupe the wounded exile and so get the weapon that is needed to take Troy, Neoptolemus tells a false tale: he was lured from home by the Greeks, who told him a "pretty story" (*kalos logos*, 353); now that his father was dead, only he could take Troy; once arrived, he was told that he could not have the weapons he had expected to get from them, because they had given them to Odysseus. Lying speeches, heroic weapons, treacherous commanders, outrages from Odysseus, all these Neoptolemus claims to share with Philoctetes. Of course he is himself using a *kalos logos* to lure his victim from "home" to Troy. We are reminded yet again of the plotters in *Electra*, ready with a persuasive story to lull their target into a false sense of security. There, the epic account of the chariot race gets the royal couple to let down their guard; here, it is Philoctetes who accepts the lies and thus opens himself to the machinations of his enemies.

Next comes a single strophe from the chorus—in place of the usual two-line comment following a long speech—which will be answered with an antistrophe only after an interval of 104 lines, a structure unique to extant Sophoclean tragedy.[33] The expansion functions as a lyric exclamation point after Neoptolemus's speech, as the chorus throws itself into the job of supporting the young man's false story. Other choruses in Athenian tragedy take part in deception, but usually by keeping silent when asked. Here they seem to take some initiative, implying but not quite saying straight out that they want the earth goddess Cybele to punish the Atreidae. The agitated dochmiac meter of the song adds to its impact, placing the chorus squarely in the middle of the deception. Philoctetes is entirely taken in by the lies:

> You have sailed here with pain that signals
> clearly to me, oh strangers;
> you sing in harmony with me, so I
> know that these are the acts of Odysseus
> and the sons of Atreus. For I have seen that he
> lends his tongue to every evil word and deed,
> from which he can accomplish unjust ends.
> But I wonder not so much at this as that
> great Ajax can have been there and put up with it.

(403–11)

Neoptolemus reports that Ajax is dead. So begins an extended exchange between him and Philoctetes about the fate of various Greek heroes who went to Troy. Odysseus and Diomedes? Still alive. Nestor? Grieving for his dead son Antilochus. Patroclus? Dead. Thersites? Alas, he lives. The catalog prompts the melancholy thought, voiced by each man in turn, that the gods take the good men and let the bad ones live on (436–37; 446–52; 456–58).

The catalog of Homeric heroes functions on various levels here.[34] Neoptolemus displays his knowledge of the Trojan War as proof of his heroic authenticity, reminding Philoctetes of his genetic inheritance. Telling the truth about what happened to these men—which Achilles would endorse—is subsumed in his larger purpose, to deceive Philoctetes, thus advancing the shifty agenda of Odysseus. Philoctetes, meanwhile, continues to establish his own heroic credentials by claiming friendship with famous warriors, further distancing himself from the pathetic outcast he otherwise appears to be. Unaware of Neoptolemus's real intentions, he thinks he is cultivating the young man's aspirations to emulate his father and disavow Odysseus's clever tongue. By conjuring Ajax and other sturdy heroes, he also unwittingly supplies fodder for the young man's eventual misgivings about deceiving him. Homer's heroes continue to hover over the entire play. Within the world of the story they serve as models for behavior, as the currency in negotiations between characters. Viewed from the audience's perspective, they embody the ongoing Athenian debates about appearance and reality, about the sources of human excellence.

Deception, Stage 2: The Play's the Thing

Neoptolemus now pushes things along by announcing his imminent departure. Philoctetes plunges immediately from comradely esprit into abject begging. Invoking the young man's parents, he appeals to Neoptolemus's innate nobility:

> To men of breeding (*toisi gennaioisi*)
> baseness is hateful and fame follows generosity.
> Ugly reproach will cling to you if you leave,
> but if you take me, my son, there will come a great gain in glory,
> if I reach the land of Oeta alive.
>
> (475–79)

He goes on abasing himself: Neoptolemus can put him anywhere he won't be a nuisance to them, in the bilge, on the prow, in the stern; he only wants his father, who he fears may be dead, to see him. By invoking the father-son bond here, he keeps Achilles in the conversation, subtly playing to the young man's sense of duty to and emulation of his father. For nearly three hundred lines, there have been not two but four characters present, Neoptolemus, Philoctetes, Achilles, and Odysseus. The last-mentioned, having kept himself out of the way since the play's opening scene, will soon put his hand in more directly.

The chorus now sings the antistrophe answering their strophe at 391–402:

Pity him, my lord. He has spoken
of enduring insufferable burdens,
the likes of which may none of our friends
encounter. And if, my lord, you hate
the cruel sons of Atreus,
I would turn their evil acts into
profit for him, carrying him wherever
he wants on the well-equipped ship
and thus escaping the righteous
anger of the gods.

(507–18)

The genuine compassion the chorus voiced in the beginning of the play now is
commandeered for the deception of Philoctetes. The poisonous duplicity that
Odysseus has loosed on the island has produced an atmosphere of ambivalence
and misdirection. Authentic feelings surface in the mouths of those advancing
falsehood; true statements about the past are folded into the lies that encompass
them; noble sentiments are harnessed for base ends. And to make the ethical
footing yet more unstable, all of this cynical manipulation is ultimately in the
service of goals that will be shown eventually to reflect the will of the gods.

As Neoptolemus prepares to take Philoctetes "home," two of his sailors enter, one disguised as a merchant. Now the deception and manipulation will increase yet further, as the machinations of Odysseus begin to work from offstage. This encounter, as we remember, has been orchestrated in advance by
Odysseus, part of his master plan to get the bow of Philoctetes (123–34). We will
be offered here another play-within-a-play, but with a new twist. Neoptolemus
and the chorus have already been performing for Philoctetes and for us, winning the former's trust with a false promise to take him home. The present
scene will have the added feature of improvisation. Odysseus has sent the disguised sailor with a story that Neoptolemus has not yet heard, from which the
young man must take whatever advantage (*sumpheronta*, 131) he can.

Both the merchant and Neoptolemus are, as it turns out, quick on their feet.
The sailor has come—expecting a decent reward, he says, a nice touch—to
warn Neoptolemus: Phoenix and two sons of Theseus are coming after him, to
bring him back to Troy. It seems the Greeks have heard through prophecy that
only Neoptolemus, using his father's arms, can take Troy. Agamemnon and

Menelaus are the leaders directly responsible for this nefarious mission. But why, Neoptolemus asks, is Odysseus not heading up the detail? Because he and Diomedes are in pursuit of another man. Who? Here the sailor shows his talent for melodrama, no doubt sidling closer to Neoptolemus and asking in a stage whisper who the other fellow onstage is and cautioning the young man to keep his voice down. To which Neoptolemus answers, "Why, it's the famous Philoctetes" (575). Now we imagine more whispering, as the merchant portentously urges immediate flight. Philoctetes hears all of this of course, as he is supposed to, and asks why the man is whispering.[35] Neoptolemus makes a show of questioning the merchant sternly. Philoctetes is his "greatest friend," because he hates Agamemnon and Menelaus. He must tell them everything! The merchant, with an appropriate reluctance, tells the story of how the prophet Helenus revealed to the Greeks that they would never take Troy unless Philoctetes was with them. He exits then, having played his part well (542–626).

As he did in *Electra*, so here Sophocles has the travelers perform a little drama in order to deceive and manipulate others onstage.[36] The toxic effects of Odysseus's original duplicity are magnified by this overt playacting. Improvising—with considerable flair—plausible lies on the spot moves Neoptolemus further toward Odysseus's slippery sophistic perspective and away from his genetic inheritance. The cruelty of his false appeal to Philoctetes as a kindred spirit, joined with him in a mutual hatred of Agamemnon, Menelaus, and Odysseus, further alienates him from the noble ideal that Philoctetes sees in Achilles. The chorus' original compassion for the suffering outcast (169–79) now rings hollow in the service of deceit. As we have seen, metatheatrical effects are not new to Sophocles. But beginning with *Electra* and continuing here, the playwright seems intent on pressing (1) the connections between dramatic performance and deception; (2) the centrality of both in reaching the goals of traditional mythic narratives; and (3) the damage done to ordinary human relationships, familial and otherwise, by the pursuit of those goals.

The Numinous Weapon

As the merchant exits, the plot of Odysseus seems to be moving along smoothly. Neoptolemus has won the trust of his prey, who is ready now to leave the island:

> Isn't it terrible, my boy, that the son of Laertius
> should ever hope with his soft words to take me

on his boat to show off to all the Greeks?
No! I would sooner listen to my very worst
enemy, the snake that crippled me.
But he will say anything, do anything;
and now I know he's coming here.
Let's be off, my child, so that a great stretch
of sea will separate us from Odysseus's boat.
Let us go! Timely haste brings rest and sleep
once the work is done.

(628–39)

We see the full power of Neoptolemus's deceitful *logoi*, just before the great *ergon* that will change everything. Philoctetes busies himself with final preparations for the trip home, gathering his medicinal herbs and any spare arrows. Neoptolemus casually expresses interest in the famous bow: may he touch it?

Sophocles begins here to tap the rich symbolic potential of the bow.[37] Philoctetes received it from Herakles, who received it from Apollo. Those exchanges imbue the weapon with an ambivalent significance. It can symbolize the civilizing power of Apollo, who killed the dragon at Delphi with it and thus established his oracle there (*Hymn. Hom. Ap.*, 300–74). But that god also wielded it to rain down plague on the Greek army (*Il.* 1. 43–52). A similar duality informs Herakles's use of the weapon. And of course Odysseus is a famous archer. Philoctetes so far has used the bow as an instrument for maintaining himself at a subsistence level. Stranded and disabled on a deserted island, he has had no opportunity to display heroic agency with his inherited arms. Neoptolemus, meanwhile, has been assured by Odysseus that *he* (Neoptolemus) will take Troy with the bow. But first he must lie to and deceive Philoctetes, becoming for a time like his would-be mentor and realizing the unheroic potential of the weapon that strikes from afar.

The young man views the bow with reverence, asking if he can "touch it and kiss it, as if it were a god" (657). He yearns for it, but will take it only if it is "lawful" (*themis*) to do so. Philoctetes is willing to let his young savior handle the bow, as a token of their growing friendship:

Your words are reverent, my child, and it is lawful;
you alone have given me the power to look at this
light of the sun, to see the land of Oeta,

and my old father, and my friends; when I
lay at my enemies' feet, you raised me up
beyond their reach. Take heart.
You may touch it, then return it to me,
and boast that because of your excellence
you of all mortals have handled it.
For I myself came to have it by doing a kindness.

(662–70)

Philoctetes reinforces the idea of the bow as a sacred relic. Not only can it be the instrument for heroic force, but it may also carry the power to bind friends together, as here. Herakles gave it to Philoctetes to thank him for setting fire to his funeral pyre when he was in agony. Neoptolemus will be the next beneficiary of the bow's power, singled out for his excellence (*aretē*, 669).

It is difficult to gauge tone from such a great distance in time, but Neoptolemus's response might suggest that the generous sentiments in Philoctetes's speech are working on him:

I do not regret having come to know you as a friend;
for whoever knows how to return a kindness he has received
is a friend more valuable than any possession.

(671–73)

In *Electra*, Sophocles creates a disjunction between the goals of the traditional revenge myth and the emotional make-up and interaction of the characters onstage, played out in part through the polarity of *logos/ergon*. We can see an analogous tension developing here, as the ability of Neoptolemus to deceive and manipulate his helpless victim, necessary for the plot to succeed, is threatened by the bond developing between himself and Philoctetes. Indeed, we may go further: the very compassion toward the disabled man that Neoptolemus must show in order to win his trust also works on the young man's innate sense of honor and justice.

Here we can see Sophocles again implicitly questioning the adequacy of traditional mythical stories for addressing the emotional issues raised by the characters onstage. Indeed, the disjunction between plot and character is more pronounced here than in *Electra*. In the earlier play, we are not encouraged to invest the Orestes we encounter in the opening scene with any depth of character or emotion. His casual insouciance about the consistency of word and action contrasts strongly with the principled struggle of Neoptolemus to comply with Odysseus's duplicity. When we see the naïve generosity of Philoctetes working on him, a strong tension develops onstage. The contest for Neoptolemus's soul is part of the story from the outset, charged with a psychological depth we only begin to feel later in *Electra*, when Orestes finally sees firsthand the impact on his sister of his lies. Here both the young man and his intended victim are portrayed as being as thoughtful and passionate from the beginning, so the cost for Neoptolemus of keeping up the deception is felt to be much higher.

The two men enter the cave together, leaving the chorus an empty stage. There follows the only complete choral ode in the play, two pairs of strophe and antistrophe. The chorus begins by invoking the example of Ixion, an exemplary wrongdoer punished by an eternity on a burning wheel in Hades. So much the more terrible has been Philoctetes's fate, since he has committed neither murder nor adultery! They go on to express compassion for the wretched outcast, marooned on a desolate island, with no companion to share his pain. No wine for him, only stagnant pools of water and the food he could kill with his bow. The final stanza hails his good fortune after much suffering. He has met "the son of noble men," who will bring him back home again (674–729).

This last section creates a problem for the traditional staging of the play, which has Neoptolemus and Philoctetes offstage in the cave until the end of the ode. In that case, we wonder why the chorus endorses the false promise of Neoptolemus when they themselves have been complicit in the plan to take Philoctetes back to Troy. The difficulty can be removed simply by having the two men reenter as the chorus begins its last stanza, in which case we see that the sailors are as agile at improvisation as Neoptolemus.[38] We have assumed that they are speaking straightforwardly at the start of the ode, since they have the stage to themselves. If we change the staging, then the chorus, turning for the last time in the antistrophe, catches sight of the two men and quickly shifts back into the false narrative. But then we might expect them to address Philoctetes in the second person. Perhaps the timing is yet more delicate, as the chorus sees Philoctetes returning but pretends to be discussing his plight as if he were still absent. However we negotiate this difficulty, issues of truth and deception remain before us, maintaining the tension in the scene.

Katabasis

Now comes the dramatic center of the play.[39] Philoctetes is stricken by the strange sickness that attends his wounded foot. The dramatic energy onstage jumps as visceral suffering and inarticulate screaming replace dialogue. Physicality like this is not common onstage in Greek tragedy and its appearance here marks a striking break in tone from what we have seen so far. The deception continues for a time, as Neoptolemus pretends not to know what's wrong with Philoctetes. At first, Philoctetes claims that he is fine, afraid that the onset of his symptoms will drive his would-be rescuer away, but the pain becomes too much for him:

> I am done for, child, not able to hide
> the evil from you, ahhhh! It goes through me,
> right through me. Oh misery, misery!
> I am destroyed, child, destroyed. It eats me up, boy. Ahhhhh,
> Ohhhhhhhhhhhhhhhhhhhh!
> By the gods, if you have a sword at hand,
> Slash off the end of my foot, cut it off now!
> Do it, boy!
>
> (742–50)

In his distress, Philoctetes begs Neoptolemus to keep the bow for him until the attack passes, never letting anyone else have it. The young man assents and as Philoctetes hands it over, he tells Neoptolemus to pray to the gods lest their envy bring sorrow to him as it did to Herakles and to himself. So the magic weapon will pass to Achilles's son, its ambiguous force for good or evil soon to be realized as the young man struggles in the face of the pain he is witnessing.[40] Philoctetes reinforces this implied heroic lineage shortly afterward, when he asks Neoptolemus to burn his body, just as he himself did for Herakles, who in turn gave him the bow (799–803).[41] By drawing the young man into this series of reciprocal gifts, Philoctetes takes part in the ongoing battle for Neoptolemus's soul, pulling him away from the influence of the other famous bowman, Odysseus.

Philoctetes struggles against the pain, but finally he is overcome and passes out, sinking to the ground (820–26). Again, falling bodies are rare on stage in Greek tragedy and would focus the audience's attention on the stricken man.

The Greek word translated above as "done for" and "destroyed" is *apolōla*, which can also mean "killed." Philoctetes calls on the earth to take him, calling himself *thanasimon* (819), which can mean "belonging to death," or simply, "dead." We are witnessing a symbolic death, powerful in its dramatic effect and in its impact on the shape of the drama. Here is an *ergon* that will sweep aside all the duplicitous *logoi* that drive the plotting of the conspirators, tapping into deep and definitive mythic structures. The passage of the bow seems here to be tied to Philoctetes's own figurative journey across the boundary of life and death, as Sophocles begins to pull together the strands of his story.

The unconscious Philoctetes draws sympathy from the chorus, which begins its next ode with a prayer to sleep, "the Healer" (832). Pity for the stricken man does not, however, shake its allegiance to Neoptolemus and the plot to get the bow. They urge Neoptolemus to grab the weapon. Prompt action at the right moment (*kairos*) wins a great victory (837–38). But Neoptolemus is no longer content simply to steal the bow:

> True, he does hear nothing, but I see that we hunt
> the bow in vain, if we sail without this man.
> The garland is his; he is the one the god said to bring.
> It is a shameful disgrace to boast with lies
> of deeds (*erga*, 842) left undone.
>
> (839–42)

Neoptolemus interrupts the strophic structure of the choral ode, speaking in dactylic hexameters, the rhythm of epic and of oracles.[42] This form gives his words a somewhat formal, elevated tone, perhaps reflecting both the influence of the oracles he interprets and his heroic lineage. Philoctetes's plight has affected him, weakening his resolve to go against his natural aversion to duplicity, tapping into the Achillean impulse to passionate involvement that Odysseus has urged him to put aside in favor of detached manipulation.[43] Words, as he says, must be matched by deeds.

The chorus is undeterred, urging prompt action while the man is helpless. The god will sort out the prophecy and its outcome. He must act *lathraiōs*, "stealthily" (850), taking care to speak *kairia*, "things appropriate to the moment" (861). These sailors have absorbed completely the perspective we have seen in Orestes, the Paedagogus, and Odysseus: the urgency to act while the opportunity is ripe, unrelenting focus on fulfilling the mission, indifference to the perils of deceit as long as the right outcome is achieved. Despite their earlier genuine compassion for the suffering of Philoctetes, they, unlike their commander, do not struggle against any particular moral scruples about deceiving and using a disabled man: they just follow orders.

By having the sailors of the chorus vigorously restate the case for stealing the bow, Sophocles separates them from their captain and shines a light on his change in perspective. Further deliberation is cut short when Philoctetes awakens, blessing the light that follows sleep and those who have watched over him, compassionate beyond his expectations. Unlike the sons of Atreus, Neoptolemus is noble by nature, the offspring of noble parents (*eugenēs gar hē phusis kaks eugenōn*, 874), tolerant of his sickness and its nasty symptoms. Since it has passed for the moment, he asks Neoptolemus to raise him to his feet again, so they may head for the ship and the voyage home.

Neoptolemus expresses pleasure at seeing his friend, who he thought was dead, restored again, and urges him to stand up or let the sailors help him. Sophocles lingers on the act itself:

PHILOCTETES
Thank you, boy. But lift me up yourself, since you thought of it.
Leave them alone; they need not be burdened with the foul odor
before it is necessary. There will be trouble enough from it
living with me on the ship.

NEOPTOLEMUS
So be it. But come now and lean on me.

PHILOCTETES
Don't worry: old habit will get me up.

(889–94)

As soon as Philoctetes is on his feet, uncertainty grips Neoptolemus: now what should he do? He has lost his way (*aporon*, 897). As Philoctetes questions him anxiously, it becomes clear that he cannot any longer go against his inborn character (*phusin*, 902). He will appear to be shameful (*aischros*, 906).

The passage of the bow has come into phase here with Philoctetes's journey from life to death and back, and both occasion Neoptolemus's return to his true nature. Sophocles has drawn on the power of myth to deepen the import of the simple acts we have just witnessed onstage. Coming into possession of the famous weapon, with all of its rich symbolic power, has impelled Neoptolemus away from the baneful influence of Odysseus and toward his genetic inheritance from Achilles. At the same time, personally lifting up his suffering friend from his deathlike condition brings him into contact with one of the most universal symbols of renewal and transformation: Philoctetes, who was "dead" (742, 745, 797, 819, 884–85), has been restored to life.[44] Like the hero who travels to the underworld (861) and returns with profound knowledge to share with his mortal fellows, Philoctetes can be a catalyst for change. We see the effects of his power immediately in the transformation of Neoptolemus's perspective.

The Hero's Body

By his contact with the apparently dead body of another man, Neoptolemus—like Orestes in the presence of the urn—is brought to a new level of awareness.[45] Physically raising Philoctetes up from the ground (cf. 667–68) seems to affect the young man powerfully, pushing him finally to give in to his inborn aversion to duplicity. He does not relinquish his role in Odysseus's deception immediately. It will take some more time before he can break completely with his would-be mentor. But the transformation begins here.

Preoccupation with the disposition of the hero's body is central to the *Iliad*, a poem always crucial to Sophocles's vision of the tragic hero.[46] Books 16–24 are dominated by the specter of the hero's unburied corpse, beginning with Zeus's ruminations over the fate of Sarpedon in Book 16, continuing as a connecting thread through the deaths of Patroclus and Hector, the funeral of Patroclus, and the final burial of Hector. By its relentless focus on the unburied body of the hero, beginning with the first lines of the proem and continuing through the entire work, the poem keeps our attention squarely on the boundary between life and death. In doing so, it implicitly raises the central questions that animate the *Iliad* and much other Greek literature and art: What does it mean to be a creature who knows s/he must die? What is the place of human existence within the larger structures of the cosmos?

In his earliest extant plays, Sophocles draws on the Homeric precedent to focus his dramatic narrative on the hero's place in his community. In *Ajax*, the title character commands the attention of the players and audience, raging against his family and fate in the first half, lying dead onstage for the rest. The question that animates the entire work is: what to do about Ajax? A powerful and unbending figure, he fits uneasily into the community formed by the Greek army. The contemporary subtext of the play engages an analogous quandary: how and to what extent should Athenians accommodate the traditional aristocratic ideas about inherited excellence, embodied by the Homeric warrior, to the new democratic social and political structure? Polyneices's corpse has much the same function in *Antigone*. The citizens of Thebes struggle with the question of how to define the dead hero's relationship to the community, with the king insisting that he is an enemy of the state and undeserving of burial, while Antigone argues for his inclusion on religious and familial grounds. Herakles dominates the attention of his community from offstage in the first two-thirds of *The Women of Trachis*. In the play's last scene, his ravaged body lies squarely on the boundary between life and death as he struggles to control it even after death. Again, Sophocles uses the physical essence of the hero, alive or dead, to focus our attention on large questions about human existence.

As we have seen, Sophocles keeps the fate of dead heroes in the forefront of *Electra* but shifts the focus somewhat to accommodate his unusual protagonist. As part of the plotters' deception, the "dead body" of Orestes commands the stage three times, in the Paedagogus's vivid recreation of the supposed death of Orestes in a chariot race (*El.* 679–763), later when the disguised Orestes enters with an urn said to contain the ashes of the dead hero (*El.* 1098–1220), and finally in the play's last scene, where Aegisthus initially believes that the shrouded corpse of Clytemnestra is Orestes's remains (*El.* 1465–73). Electra's impassioned address to the urn, itself part of the play's metatheatrical subtext, finally breaks through Orestes's breezy indifference to his sister's suffering, suddenly leaving the heretofore glib young man at a loss for words:

> Alas, what can I say? (*legō*) Where should I go
> since words (*logōn*) fail me? I can no longer control my tongue.
>
> (*El.*1174–75)

Compare Neoptolemus's reaction to Philoctetes's "rebirth":

NEOPTOLEMUS
Ah! What should I do next?

PHILOCTETES

What is it, my boy? Where have you wandered in your words? (*logōi*)

NEOPTOLEMUS

I don't know where to turn my speech. I am lost.

(895–97)

Both young men are jarred from their comfort with deceptive *logoi* by proximity to what seem to be the physical remains of a dead hero, the embodiment of the ultimate *ergon*.[47] In *Electra*, what transfixes Orestes initially is the ruined figure of his sister, dressed in rags. But it is no coincidence that she is clinging to the urn that supposedly holds the ashes of his own dead body. It is as if the juxtaposition of her diminished body to what seems to be his ultimate physical form finally makes him feel the reality of what his *logoi* are doing to her. The scene reflects the complex interplay of appearance and reality, truth and falsehood, that has colored the entire play. The cynical appropriation by the plotters of death's power over mortals, in the service of lies, comes under scrutiny when the false remains make contact with Electra's real physical ruin, itself an emblem of her suffering at the hands of callous men. Her body maps the terrible price of male indifference, but only after it touches Orestes's "corpse."

Philoctetes draws on the same patterns of meaning but consolidates the apparent corpse with the abused hero. Once the visceral power of Philoctetes's illness is filtered through the apparent death and rebirth of his body, Neoptolemus sees his friend anew. Electra's dirge to the urn launches a recognition scene, as her brother finally sees her for who she is. Likewise, Neoptolemus recognizes Philoctetes as a suffering mortal rather than a pawn to be maneuvered in order to complete his heroic mission. The connection he makes with his suppliant echoes that of his father with Priam in *Iliad* 24. The struggle for the soul of Neoptolemus is nearly over, soon to be replaced by the preoccupation with the hero's body, specifically with *where* Philoctetes is to be. Sophocles has had this issue before us from the play's opening scene, but its significance will be much more central to the play's meaning from now on. In the first scene, Odysseus said that *sōma*, "body," without *logoi* would limit Neoptolemus's ability to deceive Philoctetes and complete their mission. Subsequent events have proved him prescient.

The Return of Achilles

The next seventy-five lines dramatize the changes that the rebirth has effected. Having displayed his symbols, Sophocles now brings to life their implications for the play through his characters. Neoptolemus channels Achilles, worried for the loss of his honor, the external sign of an internal crisis. Philoctetes asks if he is reluctant to take him on his ship because of his illness. No, it is something more fundamental:

> NEOPTOLEMUS
> Everything is repellant, when one abandons
> his true nature (*phusin*) and does things that do not fit with it.

Philoctetes hears the voice of Achilles in these words:

> PHILOCTETES
> You are like your father (*phuteusantos*) when you
> do and say things to help a worthy man.

Neoptolemus confirms the pull of his genetic inheritance:

> NEOPTOLEMUS
> I will be shown to be shameful (*aischros*);
> I have long feared this.
>
> (902–6)

Neoptolemus has begun to fear for the integrity of his *phusis*, his inborn nature, always linked in this play to Achilles. Philoctetes recognizes the famous warrior when his son "does and says" (*draias . . . phōneis*, 905) things to help a man who is "noble" (*esthlon*, 905). As Electra insists (*El.* 347–50), the harmonizing of word and deed marks a person who holds traditional aristocratic values embodied first by Achilles (*Il.* 9. 312–13). That warrior's own heroic education required that Phoenix teach him as a child to be one who showed mastery of both words and deeds (*Il.* 9. 443).

We may pause here to think about the arc of Neoptolemus's struggles with competing ethical imperatives. The first exchange between Neoptolemus and Odysseus finds the young man reluctant to endorse his would-be mentor's sophistic reasoning about ends and means. The older man works on his protégé's loyalty and obedience to authority, bringing him around to agreeing to the plot to get the bow from Philoctetes using deception. This new perspective is easier for the young man to maintain as long as he can see his intended victim from a distance, as part of his commanders' larger plan to take Troy, itself prophesied by oracles.

Once he meets Philoctetes, and the wounded man begins to emerge onstage as a former warrior, a friend and admirer of Neoptolemus's father, it becomes more difficult for the young man to maintain the detachment that is required to deceive and manipulate another person. He holds out long enough for Odysseus's influence to reappear in the disguised "merchant," with whom he improvises a convincing set of reasons why Philoctetes ought to sail with him. The improvisation marks the strongest manifestation in Neoptolemus of the attitudes urged on him by Odysseus. He and the chorus—which seems not to suffer from any remorse about its part in deceiving Philoctetes—have succeeded in winning the latter's trust and Neoptolemus actually has the bow in his hands when the sickness attacks Philoctetes.

Everything changes for Neoptolemus when he witnesses the symbolic death and return to life of his intended target. Now playacting, the product of false *logoi*, is no longer possible for the young man, as he begins to move back toward his true Achillean nature (*phusis*). Though he still tries to get Philoctetes to go along with the plan voluntarily, he can no longer lie. We have noted that the change in Neoptolemus has its analog in Orestes's recognition of his sister. There too the playing out of a dramatic scene based on lies precipitates a shift in the young man's ability to maintain his detachment from a victim of his deception. Orestes's detachment from the pain his deceit causes in Electra reaches its peak in her impassioned elegy to the empty urn and dissolves at the sight of her ruined body.

The question of whether virtue can be taught informs Neoptolemus's evolution through the play.[48] Sophocles casts the issues in a typically ironic form: Odysseus, the avatar of the Sophists, would "teach" the young man what he needs to know, but the lesson he offers is that Neoptolemus needs to put aside his desire for virtue until after they have achieved their goals through deception. Meanwhile, the opposing side of the argument, that *aretē* can only be inherited through blood, is valorized through the efforts of Philoctetes to remind Neoptolemus of his ties to Achilles. Finally, *phusis* triumphs.

Considering the scenes together highlights again the persistent function of metatheatrical playacting as the vehicle not just for fiction but for cynical manipulation of innocent people. That much is not new in Sophocles, as we have noted. But considering the function of both scenes within the architecture of their plays takes us further. In each case, metatheater marks the apogee of dangerous and corrosive alienation from the truth, in the actors and in their intended audience. As he comes to the end of an illustrious career as a playwright, Sophocles does not flinch from exposing his own misgivings about the potential for harm, to Athens and its citizens, of his life's work.

The Hero's Body (2)

The first evidence of Neoptolemus's change in perspective comes when he insists that they cannot leave without Philoctetes. The play has been ambiguous on the question of whether the oracles require Philoctetes himself to wield the bow or whether the numinous weapon alone is enough to take Troy.[49] Initially, Odysseus says that if the bow is not captured, the city cannot be taken (68–69). As part of a sales pitch to win Neoptolemus over to his plan, he goes further, saying that the young man himself is destined to take the city using Philoctetes's bow (113). His subsequent instructions leave the issue unresolved, allowing for Neoptolemus and the disguised sailor to improvise their deceptions on the spot (126–31). After Odysseus leaves the stage, Neoptolemus seems to interpret the oracles differently, including Philoctetes in the destined fall of Troy:

> As for his present sufferings,
> it must be some god's plan that
> he not bend the invincible divine weapons
> until the time comes when it is prophesied
> that the city be conquered by them.

> (195–200)

The issue is left there until the false merchant reports the supposed prophecy of Helenus, whom he says Odysseus captured and brought before the Greek commanders. In this version, reported as part of Odysseus's deceptive plan but—as we will eventually learn—actually representing divine will as Herakles will describe it, Philoctetes must be present at Troy if it is to fall to the Greeks (611–18).

As we draw near to the dramatic *peripateia* occasioned by Philoctetes's illness, the chorus at least seems to have reverted to Odysseus's original formulation. Neoptolemus gets the bow in his hands on the pretense of admiring it close up while Philoctetes gathers his belongings, the latter collapses, and the chorus assumes that they can now abscond on the ship while the stricken man lies on the ground, semiconscious (832–38). But Neoptolemus now insists that the bow is of no use without the man himself. *His* is the crown of victory; the gods said they must bring him too; they will incur a "shameful disgrace" (*aischron oneidos*, 842) if they boast with lies of a mission in fact not accomplished (839–42).

The tissue of lies and vague misdirection surrounding the reports of the prophecies at this point make certainty impossible. Sophocles could easily have made the situation clearer from the outset if it suited his dramatic purposes. He seldom, in fact, aims for transparency in such matters. The will and intentions of the gods are usually left obscure in his plays, perhaps so the audience can experience, along with the characters, the frightening indeterminacy of a life ruled by omnipotent and inscrutable forces. In any event, Neoptolemus's new resolve fits with the evolution in his attitudes we have been tracing here. The brute physicality of the illness's attack on Philoctetes's body has jolted the young man out of his detachment from genuine human suffering. To ignore the actual death that will follow abandoning Philoctetes again is not possible anymore.

Neoptolemus tries to talk Philoctetes into coming with him to Troy voluntarily. A "great necessity" (*pollē/anagkē*, 921–22) compels this course. Philoctetes is outraged and refuses to consider it, calling the young man a "most hateful masterpiece of dreadful deceit" (*pan deima . . . panourgias/deinēs technēm' echthistos*, 927–28). Is he not ashamed to have deprived a suppliant of his life? Is it a point of pride for Neoptolemus to kill a corpse, a puff of smoke, a mere phantom (946–47)? Philoctetes plays all the notes that are guaranteed to keep the pressure on his young captor, the shame he will incur, the disgraceful cowardice he displays. When he finally winds down, the chorus of sailors, who were immune before to the disabled man's suffering, now need guidance from their commander (963–64).

Neoptolemus wavers. He has been trying to save the mission, in spite of his innate aversion to Odysseus's methods. But now he has to admit that he has been feeling for some time a "strange pity" (*oiktos deinos*, 965) for Philoctetes. The latter jumps on this opening, begging for pity, urging that his captor avoid the reproach that deceiving him will bring. Neoptolemus is stuck and wishes he had never left home himself. Pressing his advantage, Philoctetes now offers the young man a way to feel better about himself:

> You are not a bad man, but seem to have come here
> having learned shameful things (*aischra*) from bad men.
>
> (971–72)

Another Achilles

After lurking out of sight for eight hundred lines, Odysseus reenters here, just in time to stop Neoptolemus from completely giving in to his better nature. A struggle ensues, with Philoctetes urging his young friend to give him back his bow and Odysseus forbidding it. Philoctetes invokes Lemnos and the ovens of Hephaestus; Odysseus counters with Zeus, "who rules this land" (989). At this point, Philoctetes moves to throw himself off a cliff but two sailors grab him.[50] This skirmish makes dramatic sense given Philoctetes's heroic temperament. Death before slavery is preferable. But the physical restraint also continues the focus on the hero's body. Where he is and will be makes all the difference.

Though physically restrained, Philoctetes now delivers a long and bitter monologue, which repays our close attention. He opens by again appealing indirectly to Neoptolemus. His hands are tied by order of Odysseus; had he his bow, they would not have been able to sneak up on him, to hunt him down (*hupēlthes . . . thērasō*, 1007), using as his shield this child, deserving better than Odysseus, a worthy ally for Philoctetes; he knows only how to obey orders; see how he suffers for his part in the deception and for Philoctetes's suffering! But Odysseus's evil mind taught this naïve young man how to be clever (*sophon*, 1015; cf. *sophos*, 119) in doing evil. Now Odysseus wants to tie Philoctetes up and drag him away from the place where he once abandoned him, friendless, alone, city-less, a dead man among the living. Would that Odysseus were dead! But the gods do nothing for Philoctetes, while Odysseus and the sons of Atreus laugh at him. Yet Odysseus only joined the Trojan expedition after being kidnapped and forced, whereas Philoctetes came of his own free will with seven ships before the generals betrayed him (1004–28). Why are they taking him now? He is nothing, a dead man. Why is he, hated by the gods, not still lame and foul-smelling to the Greeks? How can they set sail with him aboard and make offerings to the gods? Didn't they throw him away in the first place to please the gods? May they be destroyed miserably! They will indeed die for destroying him, if the gods care for justice. And he knows the gods do care for justice. The Greeks would not have come back for him, a wretched man, if not goaded by the gods (1029–39).

Philoctetes ends by again cursing his enemies: he may be pitiable, but if they are punished, he will have escaped his illness (1040–44). The scale of this tirade puts the question of what to do about Philoctetes squarely before us, to remain there until the end of the play. The prior issues of how Neoptolemus would treat his unwitting captive, and which heroic paradigm would prevail in the molding of the young man's character, have largely been settled. Achilles and his legacy have been restored at the expense of Odysseus, with all of the concomitant thematic shifts that entails. Philoctetes's use of hunting imagery recalls the play's opening scene, where he was portrayed as a dangerous, un-civilized creature, an object of curiosity to be handled with great care.[51] His present situation echoes that perspective, in that he is now bound and helpless before his captors.

At the same time, his defiant refusal to go along with the Greeks' plans, even when the otherwise sympathetic Neoptolemus urges him to do so, casts him firmly in the mold of the intransigent, self-destructive Sophoclean hero, willing to die before being humiliated.[52] We cannot now help but notice, if we have not done so already, that more than being a fervent admirer of Achilles and his legacy, Philoctetes now seems to mirror the great hero.[53] Isolated from his fellow warriors but crucial to their success at Troy, he bitterly resents the Greek commanders for their earlier treatment of him; when an embassy comes from the Greek army to try to get him back to the camp, he stubbornly refuses, even when a sympathetic friend begs him to relent. (And, of course, there is his foot trouble.) His appeals to Neoptolemus in the play have so far depended on the young man seeing that not only his present interests but also his paternal heritage should incline him toward identifying with and supporting Philoctetes. After the onset of and recovery from his illness, the bond between the two men grows yet stronger as Philoctetes seems to become another version of Achilles.

Philoctetes ends his monologue by putting the spotlight on the mysterious will of the gods, who demand that he be taken back to Troy. No matter what else happens, the fulfilling of divine will is the ultimate destination for this story, as it is for all Sophoclean tragedies. Philoctetes now thinks he knows this reality and what that means for him. Nevertheless, like so many Sophoclean heroes, he will fight against the will of the gods as long as he can. The rest of the play focuses on that struggle, articulated through disputes on stage between Philoctetes and either Neoptolemus or Odysseus. Finally the issue will be settled by the arrival onstage of a representative of divine transcendence, the deified Herakles.

After Philoctetes's long tirade, Odysseus declines to engage further, saying that they will return to Troy with bow and leave Philoctetes behind. There are other bowmen available to wield the great weapon, Teucer or Odysseus himself. He takes Neoptolemus offstage with him, to prepare the ships for departure. As a last concession to Philoctetes, Neoptolemus leaves his crew behind. Perhaps the former will relent and come with them voluntarily when the time for departure arrives (1074–80).

Heroic Music

Left onstage, Philoctetes sings a long, emotional lyric dialogue with the chorus (1081–1221). Now that the course of his dismal future seems to have been set, he sings out his miseries in an intricately structured musical exchange, first in shared strophes, then in the first instance in extant Sophoclean tragedy of a long astrophic dialogue with both actor and chorus singing.[54] After his long monologue, in which he at last emerges definitively as the hero of the play, he and we now hear the chorus' response to his bleak situation.

He begins with a version of the hero's farewell, in this case not to the sun but to his cave, both warm and ice-cold. Without his bow, he is doomed, and the cave will be witness to his death (1081–94). The audience would again be reminded of Polyphemus, blinded by Odysseus and left behind, presumably helpless to feed himself in the atomistic settlements of the Cyclopes. But Philoctetes, though disabled and alone like the Cyclops, is no longer simply a monster for whose plight we may feel a fleeting twinge of sympathy. He has established himself, in our eyes and Neoptolemus's, as a Greek warrior, a comrade, of those who went to Troy and, most importantly, of Achilles. Neoptolemus's choice to honor his father's legacy of truth-telling has freed Philoctetes from the duplicity of Odysseus, and he has now emerged once and for all as the hero of the play.

The chorus' response further valorizes the portrait. Not only is he destined
to suffer and die, but it is his fault:

> You have chosen this for yourself, ill-fated man, and
> a fortune that comes from no one greater.
> When it was possible to think clearly
> you chose to approve of the worse, rather than the better fate.
>
> (1095–1100)

Like so many of Sophocles's heroes, Philoctetes is his own worst enemy, stubbornly choosing the harder path when comfort could be found in bending to
the will of others, divine or mortal. Though it has at times been sympathetic to
his miserable plight, the chorus here takes its stand with other foils in Sophocles's drama, Ismene, Chrysothemis, and—the nearest parallel for our
purposes—the chorus of *Electra*, which chides Electra because she refuses to
bend to the will of the royal couple:

> Be careful, lest your words fly too far.
> Do you not see the acts that cause your
> present pain? Do you fall unseemly into
> sufferings of your own making?
> You have gotten an excess of evil,
> always breeding wars in your
> angry soul. Such fights cannot be won
> against the powerful—yield!
>
> (*El.* 213–20)

These sobering words come in the ode that Electra shares with the chorus right
after her opening monologue, paralleled here by Philoctetes's long soliloquy. In
each case, the hero pours out her/his soul, bitterly denouncing enemies to
whom s/he will not yield. The lyrical dialogues that follow (*El.* 121–235; *Phil.*
1081–1221), with their elaborate musical form and elevated language, dramatize
the consequences for each of staking out a lonely isolation, their voices sound-
ing against the more measured words of the chorus.

The song ends and Philoctetes exits the stage, into his cave through the
central doors. Neoptolemus returns from the shore, followed by Odysseus. To

the dismay of his would-be mentor, the young man is intent on changing course:

ODYSSEUS
Will you tell me what path you're pursuing,
turning back in such haste?

NEOPTOLEMUS
To put right what I did wrong before.

ODYSSEUS
You are saying something terrible. What did you do wrong?

NEOPTOLEMUS
Being persuaded by you and the whole army . . .

ODYSSEUS
What did you do that was not proper for you?

NEOPTOLEMUS
I conquered a man by shameful deception and trickery.

(1222–28)

The verb in Greek for "I did wrong" (1224) is *hamartanō*, with its cognate noun *hamartia*, "error," appearing in the next line. Though often translated as "to fail," its most specific meaning is "to miss the mark" with a weapon. As Neoptolemus begins to act in accordance with his changed perspective, reflecting his father's values instead of Odysseus's, we see the numinous bow making a metaphorical appearance.

The ensuing exchange establishes Neoptolemus yet more firmly on the side of traditional aristocratic values as against the sophistic views of Odysseus. Achilles's son regrets having used "shameful deceit and tricks" (*apataisin aischrais . . . kai dolois*,1228); he got the bow by acting "shamefully and not with justice" (*aischrōs . . . kou dikēi*, 1234). Odysseus, he says, is "clever by nature," *sophos pephukōs*, but says nothing "clever" (*sophon*, 1244). The dispute brings us back to the earlier exchange between the two men, when Odysseus promised that if Neoptolemus would just go along with his plan to deceive Philoctetes, he would be called "clever (*sophos*) and at the same time brave" (*agathos*, 119). At the time, this prospect was persuasive for the young man, but now he is not convinced. To Odysseus's claim that he now neither speaks nor carries out "clever things" (*sopha*, 1245), he replies: "But if my words are just (*dikaia*), they are better than clever words" (*tōn sophōn*, 1246). But how is it just (*dikaion*), says Odysseus, if you let go of what you once got through my plans? (1247–48). To which: "Having made a shameful mistake (*tēn hamartian/aischran hamartōn*) I will try to undo it" (1248–49).

Odysseus can no longer control his young companion with words and resorts to threats of violence. Neoptolemus is unmoved and after some ineffectual bluster, Odysseus retreats to the ship, where he says he will "tell the story to the whole army, who will punish you!" (1257–58). There are echoes here of the negotiations over *logos* and *ergon* that informed the opening exchanges between the two men, but now the heroic insistence on matching the two has trumped rhetorical niceties. Neoptolemus calls Philoctetes from the cave and tries to persuade him to go to Troy voluntarily. The older man has not heard the prior exchange and still does not trust Neoptolemus:

> I am afraid. I fared badly before,
> persuaded by your pretty words (*ek logōn/kalōn*).
>
> (1268–70)

Neoptolemus persists: but can't a man change his mind? Philoctetes continues to be wary: "You were just like that with words (*tois logois*) when stole my bow, persuasive, but secretly ruinous" (*atēros*, 1271–72).

Neoptolemus tries for a little longer, but it is no good. Philoctetes digs in his heels in the familiar way of Sophoclean heroes. Then to his astonishment Neoptolemus offers to return the bow. Is this another trick? The young man swears by Zeus. Just as the weapon changes hands, Odysseus reappears, villainous. He tries to bully Neoptolemus, but now Philoctetes has the bow and is just prevented by the young man from shooting his enemy (1273–1302).

The Evolving Hero

The two prominent characteristics of Philoctetes from here on—his heroic resistance to divine will, the Achillean aspect of his persona, and his physical immobility, a fact from the beginning of the play but now contrasting markedly with his heroic temperament—are the key to understanding this version of Sophocles's evolving paradigm for the tragic hero. The intersection of these two aspects of Philoctetes's character and situation prompts reflection on the problem of his agency as a hero. He has the temperament of a Sophoclean hero but not the physical means for expressing his will in the world. In this sense—as in others, as we have seen—he is quite like Electra, whose stubborn resistance to authority and unbending demand that words and deeds be in harmony fit the model of the tragic hero, but whose virtual imprisonment in the royal palace denies her any means beyond words for imposing her will on others. As we have noted, in moving from *Electra* to *Philoctetes*, Sophocles shifts the position of his immobilized hero from a figure who observes and reacts emotionally to the events arranged onstage by agents pursuing the outcome contained in the traditional myth, to one whose physical location and eventual action are essential to the fulfillment of divine will as the traditional myth dictates it. As we will see in the next chapter, the redefining of Philoctetes as hero that occurs after the onset of his illness establishes a connecting thread that runs through the final three plays.

Odysseus may be banished, but the oracles—confusing though they have been—remain. After Odysseus exits, Neoptolemus delivers a long speech detailing the prophecy of Helenus that prompted the entire expedition to Lemnos (1314–47). By returning the bow and defying Odysseus, Neoptolemus has established, with Philoctetes and with us, sufficient credibility for the report to be taken as true. Helenus, he says, has promised that if he is found to be lying, the Greeks may kill him. What we learn here will be affirmed soon by Herakles: Philoctetes acquired his dreadful illness through "divine fortune" (*theias tuchēs*, 1326); he will never be well until he returns to Troy voluntarily to be cured by the sons of Asclepius; then he and Neoptolemus together will conquer Troy with the bow.

With this unadorned narrative, we return abruptly to the familiar dynamic informing tragic stories, the clash of divine will with human choice. The destined outcome of the mission to Lemnos now looms as an apparent problem: having finally sorted out Neoptolemus's character in the context of fifth-century intellectual crosscurrents, while transforming Philoctetes from repellant monster to the play's hero, Sophocles now turns to the showdown that usually comes much earlier in traditional tragic stories. In the space of some one hundred verses, a kind of tragic shorthand, he now dramatizes the formal equivalent of

Antigone's struggle to bury her brother, Ajax's defiant suicide, Oedipus's horrifying self-discovery. In response to the prophecy, Philoctetes delivers a long
speech, stepping convincingly into the role of tragic hero: Why can he not die
and go to Hades? How can he go against the apparently friendly advice of his
young friend? But again, how can he "give in" (*eikathō*, 1352) and go with the
accursed sons of Atreus and especially with Odysseus? Is Neoptolemus ashamed
to work with such villainous men? Why not honor his original promise and
take Philoctetes home to Oeta?

A further exchange between the two men follows the monologue, with Neoptolemus still trying to persuade Philoctetes to change his mind and go to
Troy, the latter stubbornly refusing to budge (1373–1401). Finally, Neoptolemus
gives in and agrees to take Philoctetes home (1402), though he is worried about
retribution from the Greeks. Never fear, says Philoctetes: I have the bow of
Herakles and will keep them from you.

Myth and Hero

All would appear to be settled, though past experience with Sophoclean tragedy would prompt some unease in the audience: What about the traditional
myth of the fall of Troy?[55] How is what we have seen so far going to be made to
fit the expected outcome? Are Neoptolemus and Philoctetes really going to suc-
cessfully defy divine will as it has been reported in the oracles? In answer,
Sophocles brings out Herakles on the *machina* above the stage.[56] The god
speaks first to Philoctetes, then to Neoptolemus, reaffirming the imperatives of
the prophecy the latter has just reported. Philoctetes must go to Troy and be
cured; after that he will kill Paris and, with the help of Neoptolemus, take the
city. The two mortals accede, Philoctetes makes a second speech of farewell to
Lemnos, and the play ends with two lines from the chorus.

This last turn in the plot is anomalous in the extant corpus of Sophocles.[57]
The only other instance of a god on stage is Athena in *Ajax*, and we have little
evidence for the use of a *deus ex machina* in Sophocles's lost plays. Its use here
might seem to be more like the practice of Euripides, who uses the device to
ironically undercut the momentum of events on stage. When the Dioscuri an-
nounce at the end of his *Electra* the destined marriage of Electra to Pylades and
Orestes's impending trial in Athens, the audience might well wonder how the
ruined woman before them could achieve marital bliss with a heretofore silent

spear-carrier (Eur. *El.* 1238–1359). Even more troubling is Apollo's command from the *machina* at the end of *Orestes*: Electra will marry Pylades and Orestes will take as his wife Hermione, daughter of Menelaus and Helen, against whose throat Orestes is pressing a knife (Eur. *Or.* 1643–65). In both of these cases, Euripides brings in the deities at play's end to align his plot with the traditional story of Orestes's trial in Athens, the subject of Aeschylus's *Eumenides*. By doing so, he creates futures for characters that are strongly (wildly?) out of harmony with their portraits as they have developed earlier in the drama. The effect of this ironic juxtaposition is hard to define precisely, but it at least undermines the integration of characters with the motivations implied by the myth.[58]

We saw in the last chapter that the character of Electra as she appears in Sophocles's play also seems an unlikely candidate for future happiness, marital or otherwise. But the playwright does not press the issue there by bringing a god onstage to lay out subsequent events. Here Herakles's connection to the bow and thus to the myth behind the play suggests a more integral connection between the divine imperatives he delivers and what we have seen dramatized.[59] His pronouncement replicates exactly what Neoptolemus has said earlier about the oracle. Though Philoctetes has insisted that he will not let go of his animus against the Greek commanders and return to Troy voluntarily, his eventual acceding to the god's commands does not create a bizarre aberration in the character we have come to know onstage. Had he been persuaded by Neoptolemus's earnest arguments, we would not, I think, find his behavior inexplicable.[60]

The abrupt intervention has other purposes, best understood in the context of Sophocles's evolving paradigm for the tragic hero.[61] In particular, we have noted the recurrent focus on Philoctetes's physical presence, where he is or will be, what he looks like, sounds like, smells like. The play begins with the new arrivals surveying his cave and worrying about where he is. Just what part he would play in the fall of Troy remains at issue throughout the drama: would he need to be physically present or just his bow? The great turning point in the struggle for the soul of Neoptolemus occurs when Philoctetes falls to the ground in agony and loses consciousness. His visceral howling and inert body have a powerful effect on the young man, turning him away from Odysseus's perspective and toward that of his father. As the wounded man lies silent and helpless on the ground, Neoptolemus decides that to simply leave him there and take the bow to Troy will not be sufficient:

> True, he does hear nothing, but I see that we hunt
> the bow in vain, if we sail without this man.

The garland is his; he is the one the god said to bring.
It is a shameful disgrace to boast with lies
of deeds (*erga*) left undone.

(839–42)

Sophocles's heroes are marked by a self-destructive defiance of more powerful forces. Though he is confirmed as the play's hero rather later in the action than usual for Sophoclean drama, Philoctetes is no exception. He would rather die than obey the oracle and endure shame. He would seem at first to be an unlikely candidate for this role, immobilized and unable to exert his will on people and things around him. Indeed, the opening scenes of the play cast him as a monstrous curiosity, repellant and dangerous. But finally, as Neoptolemus comes to accept, Philoctetes is the one Apollo said to bring to Troy; the gods have decreed that his body be in a certain place for their will to be fulfilled. Once in Troy, he and Neoptolemus must perform certain acts, which will confirm their heroic status. But in the context of this play, *where* Philoctetes is, rather than what he does, has been the dominant preoccupation. The preemptory intervention of Herakles reflects this focus: that the god stands apart from the action, looking down from another plane of existence, preserves our sense of Philoctetes's heroic defiance within the world of the play, while at the same time getting him physically to Troy so divine will can be fulfilled, as it always is in Sophoclean drama.

Conclusion: Emerging Paradigms

The figure of Philoctetes, whose nature has come into focus only slowly through the play, shares, as we have said, many traits with Sophocles's version of Electra. Both are immobilized, lacking the physical agency we usually associate with Greek heroes. While others busily pursue the imperatives of the mythical story, often negotiating with the sophistic arguments that accompany fifth-century democracy, they are motionless guardians of traditional aristocratic values. Each stands to the side, detached from the acts of those pursuing the outcome required by the myth, but reacting emotionally to them. And the body of each finally exerts power over the more mobile plotters. Electra's ruined physical state, joined with the supposed ashes of Orestes, jolts Orestes out of his insouciant attitude toward the suffering of others. Witnessing Philoctetes driven to the ground by his wound stirs in Neoptolemus his genetic inheritance from Achilles and weakens the influence of Odysseus yet further. Both events alter the momentum of the plot, increasing the hero's participation and leverage.

In the crucial relationship between the hero's will and the destined outcome of the myth, Sophocles takes a step further in *Philoctetes*. Whereas both Electra and the plotters are certain that they are in harmony with divine will, Sophocles declines to settle the matter, leaving the end of the play murky. Philoctetes, by contrast, is to be—along with Neoptolemus and the bow—the instrument for the fall of Troy. The shifting reports in the early part of the play on whether Philoctetes himself must be in Troy or only his weapon add energy to the question of where he will end up. These latter two innovations look forward to Sophocles's last play. The aged Oedipus, blind and dependent on the kindness of strangers, will be moved around the stage by others, his body the focus for the wrangling over the outcome of various prophecies. In him, Sophocles—himself a very old man—reimagines the relationship between divine will and human choice, always at the heart of Greek tragic literature, and concludes his profound portrait of the place of human experience in the larger structures of the cosmos.

CHAPTER 4

Oedipus at Colonus

Spiritual Geography[1]

A March afternoon, the Theater of Dionysus, twenty-five hundred years ago. From the audience's left, two figures appear, making their slow and careful way down the *eisodos* in the slanting sunlight. His staff and shuffling gait identify one as the aged Oedipus, blind and leaning on his daughter Antigone. The old man speaks:

> Antigone, child of this blind old man, what
> land have we reached, whose city?
> Who will receive the wandering Oedipus with
> paltry gifts today? Seeking a pittance, I have
> even less, and that is enough for me.
> Suffering and time, long my companion,
> and nobility too, teach me to be content with these gifts.
> But do you see a place to rest, my child,
> on unhallowed ground or in the grove of the gods?
> Stop and sit me down there, so we may learn
> where we are. For we have come as strangers
> to learn from citizens and do what they say.
>
> (1–13)

Those sitting on the slope of the Acropolis might well have wondered if the actors were performing the play backwards.[2] The hero—an unlikely one in any event—enters proclaiming that he intends to take instruction from the locals. He has learned patience and asks for little. A Sophoclean hero might eventually arrive at this abject state after failing to impose his or her will on others (though a noble suicide would usually preclude this scene of self-abasement), but we do not expect him to make his first appearance in this condition.[3] That the play opens thus begs a question: where will the plot go from here? If the hero enters already broken by his/her life, it would seem that the usual emotional arc of a tragic story—arrogant overreaching fed by pride leads to crisis, wherein the hero must choose to bend his/her will to forces beyond mortal control or face destruction, at his/her own hands or by others—is not available. Oedipus will seek his own death, we soon learn, but not out of despair. It has been prophesied, like many a hero's death, but he will go to meet it triumphantly. By obeying the will of the gods, he will be awarded a "great consummation" (*perasin . . . katastrophēn,* 103) to end his life.[4]

Viewed through the lens we have been using in the previous chapters, this hero looks somewhat more familiar. Blind and physically frail, Oedipus, like Philoctetes, lacks the usual heroic agency for imposing his will. Like both Electra and Philoctetes, he is immobile, while travelers with self-serving agendas try to use him for their own purposes. He, meanwhile, remains detached from their imperatives, which reflect the urgencies of traditional myths. Though disabled, his body, like those of the earlier two heroes, will exert power over others and be a conduit for the will of the gods. Much will depend, as in *Philoctetes,* on the location of his body, which the various travelers work to move. And as they do so, the Theater of Dionysus will become a landscape symbolizing various geographies, physical and spiritual. In his last play, we will see Sophocles gathering the threads of his new conception of heroic agency into a final tapestry, his own great consummation.

Mapping the Past and Future

Recent work on the staging of Sophoclean drama has provided new dimensions for the study of the plays.[5] David Wiles has noted that *Oedipus at Colonus* in particular seems to be articulated in the theater by what he calls "lateral opposition."[6] That is, horizontal movement by the actors can be understood to mark various kinds of polarities—temporal, geographical, and spiritual.[7] The consensus of scholarly opinion has the *eisodos* to the audience's left (stage right) lead toward Thebes, that on the audience's right, toward Athens;[8] on the right side of the orchestra is an equestrian statue, with a grove of trees on the left. The central doors of the *skēnē* would lead into the sacred grove of the Eumenides, where Oedipus is destined to end his life; just outside them would be some kind of stone or ledge to sit on; a large stone in the center of the orchestra would provide another resting place. The Theater of Dionysus was situated at the foot of the Acropolis, with the slope used for seating. The audience would be looking south at the orchestra and *skēnē*, the front of which faced north, with the March sun moving generally from their left (Thebes, east) to their right (Athens, west). Figure 1 below illustrates this setting:

SOUTH

Grove of the Eumenides

Skēnē

(ledge)

Eisodos: left	*Eisodos: right*
Thebes	Athens
Grove of trees	Equestrian statue

EAST   **Stone**   WEST

Audience

Acropolis

NORTH

Already we can see various levels of meaning in this allotment of space. Thebes will, as usual in Athenian tragedy, represent the "anti-Athens," repository of dark, disturbing desires and base motivations. Athens, meanwhile, will hold out the promise of sanctuary for a wandering, needy suppliant, a locus for compassion and hope, as embodied in its noble king, Theseus.[9] Moving toward Thebes takes Oedipus back to his ruinous past, while Athens beckons him toward future redemption. The left exit leads offstage into the country, toward not only Thebes but Mount Cithaeron, site of Oedipus's infant exposure—his "mountain mother," as the chorus of *Oedipus Tyrannos* calls it (1091)—the place where he begs to be left again at the end of that play, a wild venue for his monstrous condition. To the right lies Athens with its great civilization, a bulwark against the unnatural forces released by Oedipus's past behavior.

Finally, as others try to pull him back and forth across the stage, Oedipus veers between anger and defiance—the result of contact with his past—and the meek, frail passivity he displays in the opening scenes. That he opts in the end to be buried near Athens has him moving in concert with the path of the sun across the Theater of Dionysus. His final exit through the central doors of the *skēnē* marks his transcendence of the tension between these extremes, as he taps the power of the gods to lead the way into the grove and his mysterious disappearance.

Antigone eases Oedipus onto the ledge in front of the *skēnē*. As they reconnoiter, recognizing Athens in the distance, a citizen of Colonus (ironically called *xenos*, "stranger") enters from the audience's right. He dismisses Oedipus's initial question:

OEDIPUS
Stranger, I hear from this girl, who
sees for me and for herself, that you have
come to question us at the right time to clear things up . . .

STRANGER
Before you inquire further, leave this seat!
You occupy ground on which it is unholy to walk.

(33–37)

A further exchange affords details about the immediate area: Oedipus sits on the "Brazen-footed Threshold," on the edge of a grove sacred to the Eumenides, "dread goddesses, daughters of Earth and Darkness" (39–40); Oedipus declares that he will not ever leave the place, which he says rather cryptically is the "sign of my destiny" (46); the entire place is sacred (*hieros*, 54) to Poseidon and to Prometheus; the equestrian statue is of Colonus, eponymous founder of the nearby community.

Now the *skēnē* and its mysterious interior are marked, a further articulation of the spiritual geography on stage. Oedipus sits on the edge of eternity in more than one way. He straddles the boundary of space controlled by immortals and so fosters anxiety in the locals; at the same time, he himself is approaching the end of his mortal existence and has been invited by prophecy to cross over into the undiscovered country of the dead. Finally, like all Greek tragic heroes, he functions for us as the agent for exploring the boundaries that define human existence.

Back from the Edge

The citizen bustles off to find other locals, who will decide if the blind stranger should be allowed to remain. As soon as he is gone, Oedipus launches into a passionate prayer to the Eumenides, begging for their sympathy. Apollo, it seems, has told him in a prophecy that he is to end his wanderings in their grove, the "final place" (*chōran termian*, 89) where he will find rest and shelter, the goal of his long-suffering life. By doing so, he will bring "profit" (*kerdē*, 92) for those who receive him and destruction for those who sent him away. The gods will send signs of this destiny, an earthquake, thunder, or lightning. He concludes with exhortations to the "sweet daughters of ancient darkness" and to Athens, "the most honored of cities" (106–10).

The chorus, old men from Colonus, make their initial entrance down the right *eisodos*. Antigone spies them, quickly leading Oedipus through the doors of the *skēnē* and out of sight for the moment. The elders are agitated:

> Look! Who was he? Where does he live?
> Where has he rushed off to, most
> shameless of all, of all?
> Look! Speak out!
> Seek him out everywhere! A wanderer,
> the old man is a wanderer, not a
> native!
>
> (118–25)

They have been told that this stranger has transgressed the ground sacred to the Eumenides and has broken the silence that must surround the site. Oedipus and Antigone emerge from beside the entrance to the grove at the end of the first strophe, causing further upset:

CHORUS
Ah, ah!
He is terrible to see, terrible to hear!

(140–41)

The word for "terrible" here is *deinos*, a richly suggestive adjective the full impact of which is not easy to reproduce in English.[10] Certainly the old stranger looks and sounds bad: years of wandering have taken their toll on his body; his voice we imagine to be thin and reedy. But this context imbues the chorus' words with much greater weight. To be *deinos* is to inspire awe, to take others aback. Such a person is dangerous, to be handled with great care. (We are reminded of the sailors' fear of encountering Philoctetes, another frightening creature, for the first time.) The word is used of Achilles, of Medea, angry, numinous creatures.[11] Oedipus will be all of this and more before he walks through those doors again.

Oedipus begs them not to see him as *anomos*, "lawless," but the chorus remains skeptical. Who is this old man? Oedipus assures them that he is not one to be envied, blind and depending as he does on a small girl (142–49). In the first antistrophe, the chorus' alarm increases. While they pity the stranger's sad life, they worry that he may bring down curses on them by transgressing on sacred ground. He "goes too far, too far" (*peras gar/peras*, 155–56). If he wants to speak to them, he may do so, but first he must leave the grove.

Now begins the painstaking process of moving Oedipus across the stage:

ANTIGONE
Father, we must share the cares of the citizens,
yielding and obeying when necessary.

OEDIPUS
Now put your hand on mine.

ANTIGONE
Yes, I am touching you.

OEDIPUS
Oh strangers, let me not suffer wrong,
trusting in you as I move.

CHORUS
Never, old man, will anyone lead you
from this seat against your will.

OEDIPUS
Further then?

CHORUS
Still further forward.

OEDIPUS
Further?

(171–80)

The laborious process goes on for another twenty-two lines, until the chorus and Antigone finally get Oedipus to the rock at the center of the orchestra. The entire second strophe and antistrophe are contained within this anxious exchange, with the chorus, Oedipus, and Antigone sharing the lines in a complex lyric dialogue. A long epode follows (207–36), sung by Oedipus and chorus, and finally a lyric solo by Antigone (237–55). Sophocles continues the practice he began in *Electra*, of a *parodos* shared by the chorus with one or more actors. The combined effect of physical motion and lyrical singing would be striking, drawing the audience's attention to the old man's slow progress across the stage, freighted with meaning on various levels.[12]

First Reckoning

Now that Oedipus is safely removed from sacred space, the chorus gets down to business: Who is he? Where is he from? Oedipus tries to deflect their curiosity: "Oh strangers, I am an exile (*apoptolis*), but do not . . ." (207). The chorus persists, and he becomes increasingly desperate:

No, no, do not ask me who I
am; do not seek to examine me further!

(210–11)

After further prodding, it all comes out:

OEDIPUS
Do you know a son of Laius?

CHORUS
Oh! Ah, ah!

(220)

The chorus is reduced to inarticulate groaning by this news and orders him to leave immediately. When Oedipus reminds the old men of their earlier pledge not to drive him away against his will, they reply that things have changed. By deceiving them about his identity and origins, he has forfeited their protection. He must "leap forth" (*ekthore*, 234) from their land, before he brings some further burden on their city. In the eyes of these earnest citizens, Oedipus is the same man he was at the end of *Oedipus Tyrannus*, a onetime hero stained with patricide and incest. As far as they are concerned, contact with him can only bring harm to Athens.

This moment is Oedipus's first contact in the play with his past. He will not be able, it seems, to remain anonymous if he is to be taken in by Athens as a suppliant. Other Greek heroes rely on their past histories to provide them leverage in the form of *kleos*. For them, being known by others usually brings power. When Odysseus announces his name in the *Odyssey*, his status always rises. In this, as in other ways, the old Oedipus departs from the normal pattern of Greek heroism. Past deeds will afford no relief to the old wanderer. Nor will running away suffice. He will have to face the horrors in order to finally transcend them. In doing so, he will be drawn back toward Thebes, tugged at by its representatives, Creon and then Polyneices. Facing them will bring out a different Oedipus, angry and defiant, not passive and meek.

After Antigone pleads for mercy, Oedipus revisits his past with a spirited self-defense. What good is Athens' fine reputation for reverence to the gods and kindness to strangers, if they now drive him away simply out of fear of his name? They surely cannot be afraid of his physical body (*sōma*, 266) or his actions. In the matter of his parents, he did not act but rather was acted upon; he only struck in self-defense, so even if he had known they were his parents, he would still not be evil by nature (*kakos phusin*, 270); as it is, he was entirely ignorant, while those who knew better destroyed him.

We return here to the issues crucial to the moral universe of *Oedipus Tyrannus*. Viewed now from some remove, Oedipus's past acts, however appalling in their implications, carry less of the visceral horror that dominates the end of that play. His self-defense here is at least plausible—though not surprisingly, the arrogance that fueled his youthful decisions goes unremarked. But finally, however knotty the moral and ethical problems raised by Oedipus's past are, they will not be the principal focus of this play. As in *Electra*, the central character, by force of personality, pulls our attention away from familiar issues found in traditional stories. We will see that Oedipus eventually steps away from the entire context of the Theban stories, breaking his attachment to his dark past and moving confidently into the undiscovered country of the dead.[13]

Having offered his self-defense, Oedipus urges the chorus to shift its attention away from his terrible history. As representatives of Athens, the old citizens must honor the gods, whose gaze falls upon the pious and the impious man alike. No unholy man (*phōtos anousiou*, 281) has ever escaped judgment. They have received him as a suppliant and must not dishonor him when they look on his unsightly face. Now comes a startling claim:

> For I have come as a reverent and sacred man (*hieros eusebēs*), bearing
> profit (*onēsin*) for the citizens here; and whenever the man
> in power arrives, whoever is your ruler,
> then you will hear and understand everything.
> Meanwhile, by no means be cruel.
>
> (287–91)

That Oedipus, an incestuous parricide, can claim to be sacred[14] alerts us that something extraordinary is afoot. And what profit could such a man offer to a city like Athens? By the end of the play, Oedipus will demonstrate the truth of both claims, embodying a kind of heroic persona not seen before in the Theater of Dionysus.

Sophocles heads into new territory in these first scenes, but he travels as usual with material from his earlier plays. We note, for instance, some parallels with *Philoctetes*: a sacred precinct transgressed; the disabled hero's shunning and exile; the chorus' anxious desire to avoid contact with a man who appears to be dangerous to its members, balanced by their curiosity about him; the hero's subsequent attempt to rehabilitate himself in the eyes of others who could release him from his suffering. For both men, others' perception of the past is crucial for reestablishing some sense of self-respect. Philoctetes hopes that by invoking his former friendship with various men who fought at Troy, he can make Neoptolemus see him as a fellow warrior, not as a repellant, disabled creature. For Oedipus, invoking the past will only prolong his exile. His goal is to convince the citizens that though he seems repulsive they should ignore his history and concentrate on the present, his status as suppliant, and the future, when the "profit" he promises can be realized.[15]

The chorus' visceral revulsion at discovering Oedipus's identity and ruined condition, combined with his surprising claim to be "sacred," form the matrix of Sophocles's evolving paradigm for heroism. The blind old man has become something of a holy monster, his tainted past and physical decrepitude belying the fact that he has been singled out by the gods to be the vehicle for their power, a shattered yet mysteriously potent vessel. We saw in Electra the beginnings of this new conception, a bitter, worn-out woman whose physical appearance horrifies her brother. The opening scenes of *Philoctetes*, invoking the Cyclops episode from the *Odyssey*, continue the paradigm, as the chorus fears the return to its lair of the primitive, foul-smelling creature. Nevertheless, as we soon learn there, this unlikely hero has been chosen by the gods to be the instrument for the fall of Troy. We have traveled far from Achilles, physically beautiful and semidivine, the obvious representative of heroic excellence. To accept this new kind of hero will require us to expand our understanding of the sources of human excellence and its place in the larger play of forces in the tragic universe.

Turning toward Thebes

Another traveler appears, who will pull Oedipus back toward his past. Antigone spots Ismene off in the distance in a Thessalian sun hat, riding toward them from Thebes. She enters with news of his sons, for whom things are bad. Oedipus replies that they are unworthy, living like Egyptian men, who sit at home while their wives go out to work. While they fight over the kingship, his two daughters have taken up the responsibility of caring for him, Antigone wandering with him, Ismene serving as his source for news from Thebes (339–60). Ismene reports that Eteocles, the younger son, has ousted Polyneices and seized the throne. The latter has married and raised an army in Argos, preparing to attack his brother. Amid all this bad news there is one ray of hope:

OEDIPUS
Have you found any hope that the gods
will look at me, so I might be saved someday?

ISMENE
I have, father, from the newest prophecies.

OEDIPUS
What prophecies? What has been foretold, child?

ISMENE
That you will one day be sought by those people there,
in death and in life, for the sake of their salvation.

OEDIPUS
Who would do well through such a man as I am?

ISMENE
They say that their power will rest with you.

OEDIPUS
When I no longer exist, then am I a man?

ISMENE
Yes, because now the gods lift you up, who destroyed you before.

(385–94)

Creon, Ismene goes on to say, will come soon to try to move him back near
Thebes. Not inside the city, since he is still ritually unclean, but close by so they
can watch him: if something goes wrong with his tomb, it will be trouble for
them. This "trouble" (*kaka*) will come "from your anger, when they encounter
your tomb" (411).

The struggle to move Oedipus's body comes to the fore again. Creon will
embody the dark pull of Oedipus's Theban past, realized by leftward movement
across the stage, to be counterbalanced by the rightward tug of Theseus, noble
king of Athens. And in the middle of the *skēnē*, the mysterious consummation
that beckons from the grove. The opening of the play, as we will see, offers a

symbolic representation of the entire drama: Antigone carefully bringing her father on stage and seating him at the entrance to the grove, then the laborious process of moving him again, away from his eventual salvation, vulnerable again to the pull of those forces that seek to control him. It will be a long journey back to the threshold, encompassing the old man's dark past, anxious present, and mysterious future.[16]

Oedipus continues to fill in his past history, while venting his anger at his sons. He hopes the gods will not end their quarrel, that he may be granted the decision as to its outcome: let Eteocles be ousted from the throne and Polyneices remain in exile, a fit reward for their abandoning of him. Right after discovering the truth of his identity and its horrifying consequences, he wanted only to be stoned to death; time passed and his self-loathing eased, but then the city decided to drive him out and his sons did nothing to help him! Only his daughters were loyal, following him into exile and caring for him while his sons fought for power. But there will be a reckoning:

> They will gain nothing from me as an ally,
> nor get any profit (*onēsis*) from the Theban kingship.
> I know this, from hearing this girl's prophecies
> and from interpreting the ancient oracles
> that Apollo has at last fulfilled.
>
> (450–54)

He ends defiantly with a pledge: let Creon come or anyone else they choose. If the Athenians are willing, with the help of the dread goddesses of the grove, to give him protection, they will win a great protector (*sōtēr*, 460) and bring trouble to his enemies.

A different version of Oedipus is emerging from the frail, passive old man who entered with Antigone. He claims to be "sacred" and promises to become a "savior" for Athens, who will bring "profit" (*kerdē*, 92) to them if they will give him sanctuary. The source of his new leverage will be the gods, of whose power his shattered body will be the unlikely vehicle. We noted that from his first entrance in the play, Oedipus presents an atypical profile for tragic heroes, marked by patient acceptance rather than the usual expression of heroic will in defiance of larger forces. Now we begin to see that far from being powerless, the old man has been chosen, for mysterious reasons, to channel the force of divine will.[17]

The full impact of this numinous persona will be fully realized, it seems, only after Oedipus's death, when the profit he promises will be awarded. Meanwhile, turning toward Thebes and his troubled past animates the old man. At the grove's edge he was awaiting instructions from other mortals, happy to be given even less than he already had, meek and passive. News about his sons and their quarrel brings not paternal solicitude but angry denunciation, as the heroic will so prominently on display in *Oedipus Tyrannus* reappears.

The chorus draws Oedipus's attention back to the grove of the Eumenides and his present situation. If he is truly to be the city's protector, they suggest that he perform a purification ritual (*katharmon*, 466) for the deities of the grove. He eagerly asks for more guidance and there follows another outpouring of minute instructions from the citizens: libations from a stream, poured with pure hands from approved basins, the fleece of sheared lambs, facing east, and so forth. Oedipus enlists his daughters to perform the rites, as his frailty and blindness prevent him from doing so. But they must not leave him entirely alone:

> For my body (*demas*) lacks the strength
> To move alone or without a guide.
>
> (501–2)

The acquiescent stranger, ready to follow the lead of others, has returned for the moment, supplanting the angry father.

Kings Bearing Gifts

Ismene exits to perform the necessary ritual acts, leaving Oedipus, Antigone, and the chorus on stage. Moving the action offstage after such an elaborate build-up makes this moment feel like an interlude, the obvious time for a choral stasimon. Instead, there follows a complex lyric dialogue in strophic form between Oedipus and the chorus.[18] Short phrases and emotive outbursts from both sides are fitted into the strophic structure, with some single lines of verse shared (*antilabē*), a technique first used, as we noted, in *Electra* (*El.* 823–70). The chorus, sensing that they have the old man at their disposal while the rituals are performed offstage, prod for more details about his past:

It is terrible (*deinon*) to stir up evil long dormant, oh stranger,
but all the same I'd like to know . . .

(510–11)

Oedipus begs them in the name of hospitality not to press him, but the elders
persist: the story is everywhere anyway, so why not give us your version? Oedipus is at first reduced to cries of anguish but then stiffens, laying out his self-defense in response to the chorus' relentless prodding. He endured evil by his
own will, but none of it was by his own choice (*authaireton ouden*, 522). The city
"bound" him (*enedēsen*), ignorant though he was, in an evil wedlock (525–26).
The murder of his father and incestuous begetting of his children were likewise
done in ignorance. He *suffered* evil but did not *do* evil (*epathon . . . ouk ereksa*,
538–39). He elaborates on this last distinction:

> I received
> a gift (*dōron*), wretch that I was, which I
> never should have taken.

(539–41)

Gifts, as we will see, figure largely in the articulation of Oedipus's legacy to
Athens.

Here, as in his earlier self-defense, Oedipus's claims of innocence before the
law rest on his past ignorance, a poignant admission for the onetime king so
proud of his intellectual gifts. But though the thrust of his argument is the same
as before, the form it takes, the vivid, rapid-fire nature of this sung dialogue
increases the emotive force of his claims. Rather than lowering the dramatic
tension with a more detached choral song, Sophocles increases it with this virtuoso passage. Beginning with his first self-justification to the chorus, continuing in the reports about his sons' predicament, and now in this intense dialogue, the presence onstage of Oedipus's problematic past has grown. As he
struggles to move toward the final destiny the oracles have predicted, his old
heroic existence, with all its ambiguous moral baggage, threatens to pull him
back. At the same time, his obvious pain at recalling it all, and the mix of shame
and defiance he exhibits in the face of it, bind the story's past inextricably to the
battered figure presently onstage before us. Sophocles invites us to revisit the
wrenching conflicts of his earlier play, but not in order to settle, once and for all,

the moral tangles of that work. Rather, their meaning in this play is always as a part of the presentation of *this* Oedipus in *this* dramatic moment.

Theseus finally arrives and recognizes Oedipus immediately from his shabby appearance and unhappy face. As someone who himself was raised in exile and struggled against dangers throughout his life, he feels a connection with the old man and is inclined to grant whatever Oedipus asks:

> . . . since
> I know I am a man, and have no more
> power over what tomorrow brings than you.
>
> (566–68)

The humility and compassion Theseus shows here confirm his role as the embodiment of Athenian greatness, with its admirable record of receiving and protecting suppliants.[19] Thebes and its discontents have grown more visible onstage, but now a powerful ally from the present appears. Though the chorus of elders has treated the wandering stranger with watchful courtesy, Theseus now supplies the necessary authority to shore up the defenses against aggressive agents from abroad, soon to appear.

Oedipus returns Theseus's generosity with appropriate deference. (Is there perhaps a hint of humor in his declaration that Theseus's display of his own nobility has left Oedipus with nothing to add?) Encouraged by his host, he proceeds briskly to the main business:

> I have come to offer this my wretched body (*demas,* 576)
> to you, a gift (*dōron*) not comely to look at; but from it will come
> benefits (*kerdē*) that are better than a beautiful form.
>
> (576–78)

Oedipus is a suppliant, who must depend on the kindness of strangers.[20] The gift he offers in return, however, would seem not to be especially valuable. What profit will your gift bring, Theseus politely inquires. He will have to wait to learn, until they bury Oedipus's dead body. In response to further questioning, Oedipus reveals the full story: the Thebans' need to control his body and grave so as to ward off future destruction, the gods' role in compelling them, his own sons' treacherous complicity in his exile from Thebes. Theseus, though sympathetic, cannot see how the Thebans and his sons can cause bitterness for *him* (579–606).

In answer, Oedipus delivers a lyrical meditation on the irresistible power of "all-conquering time" in the affairs of mortals:

> The power of the land withers, like the strength of bodies;
> trust dies and treachery is born;
> the same spirit endures between neither men
> nor cities, since sweet agreement
> turns to bitterness, then is restored,
> for some who live now and others later.
> If all is fair weather now, for you and the Thebans,
> yet time runs on without end, giving birth
> to days and nights in which they will shred
> with spears your harmonious pledges,
> and for petty reasons.
> Then my buried corpse, cold and
> slumbering, will drink their hot blood down . . .
>
> (607–22)

The lines are reminiscent of Ajax's beautiful but deceptive speech before killing himself, where heroic defiance seems to have yielded finally to the overpowering forces of time and nature (*Aj.* 646–77). There the sentiments mark only an apparent turnabout. Not so here. Oedipus has waited long for his life's fulfillment, suffering loneliness and exile. Not for him the search for *kairos*, the right moment for heroic action. He has come to see time as punctuated not by the plans of mortals but by the slow, cyclical rhythms of nature, calling for endurance, not active assertion. Theseus, the benign exemplar of traditional heroism in the play, thinks in terms of being thwarted in the expression of his will as protector. Oedipus, denied the usual heroic agency, focuses instead on the extra-human, transcendent forces that will finally control what mortals like to think of as their self-expression. He too will be a protector for Athens, but as one part of a larger system in which he has a part to play.[21]

The exchange with Theseus brings together several qualities that link the old Oedipus to both Electra and Philoctetes. Both of the earlier heroes share his attitude toward time. All three endure the manipulation of others, waiting for their lives to gain meaning through suffering. In regard to their bodies, there is in all three a sense of inwardness, latency, even gestation, which replaces the usual outward thrust of heroic will. Electra is said to "give birth to war in her soul" (*El.* 218–19); Philoctetes's wound is always ready to burst forth with pus, oozing infection from inside; Oedipus, blind and led around by children, recalls Teiresias in *Oedipus Tyrannus*, who "nourishes" (*trephō*, *OT* 356) truth inside himself; like the prophet, he is the vehicle for giving birth to the will of the gods. In all three plays, the issue of "profit" (*kerdos* or *onēsis*) figures prominently. Orestes, Clytemnestra, Odysseus, Neoptolemus, and Oedipus all meditate frequently on what will bring profit or advantage to them or others. That Oedipus offers profit to the Athenians in the form of his dead body, which he sees as a gift guaranteed not by him but by the gods, suggests an entirely different conception of how mortals can contribute to their own and others' well-being.

Despite Oedipus's dire warnings about the seriousness of the struggle (*agōn*, 587) he is entering, Theseus promises that no one will harm the old man once he is under the protection of Athens. He may go with Theseus, or stay in the care of the locals. Oedipus opts for the latter, wanting to remain close to the grove. Theseus exits to perform a sacrifice and the chorus sings its first stasimon, one of Sophocles's most famous odes, a song of praise for the natural beauty of Colonus and, indirectly, for Athenian greatness. Theseus's treatment of Oedipus and promise of protection find their musical equivalent in the tranquility of the song and its emphasis on what will endure beyond the disputes of mortals—the Greek word *aei*, "always," "forever," appears frequently.[22] Athens is called "the gift (*dōron*) of a great god" (710), echoing Oedipus's own claims to Theseus earlier.[23]

Attack on the Left Flank

The mood is shattered immediately by the arrival, from the audience's left, of Creon with his retinue. We have heard of this old man's nefarious plans and expect a villain. Creon does not disappoint. Though presumably even older than Oedipus, he displays a vigorously malign attitude toward his nephew/brother-in-law.[24] Beginning with smarmy praise of Athens' greatness and phony solicitude for Oedipus, he moves swiftly to shaming:

It is painful to see your sorrows, old man,
exiled as you are, a wandering beggar, indigent and stumbling,
leaning on just one companion. And I am wretched seeing her,
who I never thought would fall to such depths of misery,
a miserable beggar herself. Always caring for you and your body (*kara*,
    750),
living a beggar's life, knowing nothing of marriage—even at her age,
prey to being snatched by a passerby.

(744–52)

Shame is the common coin of heroic culture. Appearing inadequate to one's peers is to be avoided at all costs, as attested by Ajax's suicide. This approach by Creon confirms again that Thebes is to be identified with Oedipus's heroic past, tainted by willful arrogance and pride. In Theseus and now Creon, Sophocles has embodied each of the poles between which Oedipus's destiny oscillates in the play.[25]

Facing his past again animates Oedipus and he replies scornfully: why does Creon, who will stoop to any clever trick (*mēchanēma poikilon*, 762), try again to snare him in the kind of trap that would bring him the most pain? The Thebans only want him to avoid trouble for themselves, not out of any solicitude for him. He is a clever speaker whose words sound good, but in fact are evil (*logōi men esthla, toisi d'ergoisin kaka*, 782; see also *glōssēi . . . deinos*, 806).[26] He ends with a threat: the Thebans want to escape harm by controlling his grave, but they will instead have his vengeful spirit (*alastōr*, 788) living near Athens forever; his sons can inherit only enough of his country to die in (785–90).

Familiar themes begin to surface here. Cast by Oedipus in the role of clever, deceptive speaker, Creon recalls Orestes and the Paedagogus in *Electra* and the Odysseus of *Philoctetes*, manipulating others for their own gain, depending on *logoi*, concealing the true nature and import of their *erga*.[27] The hunting imagery in Oedipus's initial rhetorical questions echoes the opening scene of the latter play, where devious visitors plot to ensnare the repellent creature in the cave (cf. *Phil. 1007*). Like the choruses in the previous two plays, Creon suggests that the hero's behavior is self-destructive: he is only hurting himself (*El.* 215–20; *Phil.* 1095–1100). The insults fly back and forth, until Creon plays his trump card: he has Ismene and will soon capture Antigone (819–20). Oedipus's defiance vanishes, as he begs the chorus to help him.

The stand-off continues for seventy lines, with threats of violence and perhaps some physical action, as the chorus tries unsuccessfully to prevent Creon's henchmen from dragging Antigone away. As when Oedipus is moved slowly across the stage earlier, Sophocles here uses lyric dialogue, shared by Creon, Oedipus, Antigone, and the chorus, to increase the dramatic energy onstage. Lines 833–43 form a strophe, answered by the antistrophe at 876–86. The meter is a mix of dochmiacs, always associated with high emotion, and iambic trimeters. Between are thirty-two lines of spoken dialogue in iambic trimeters. The entire passage is articulated through short, staccato phrases, with speakers sharing lines, representing anger, fear, and mounting panic. The old men cannot protect Antigone, and Creon is about to have his men drag Oedipus away when Theseus returns to restore order.

Athens to the Rescue

Theseus enters somewhat agitated: What is this shouting about? What scared you into disturbing my sacrifice to Poseidon? I've hurried over here faster than is enjoyable for my feet (886–90). There is a hint of something like parental reproof in the king's words. The arguing has taken him away from serious duties, and it had better be over something important. The effect would be to undermine the status of both Creon and Oedipus, making their quarrel appear to be more like ill-tempered bickering between siblings. (Those familiar with Sophocles's earlier plays might see a parallel with Jocasta's rebuke of Oedipus and Creon at *OT* 634–38.) How much weight this tone might have here, or how it is meant to influence our perception of the two combatants, is hard to judge. Certainly it increases Theseus's stature and authority, as he imperiously dispatches troops to guard the crossroads where the two daughters would pass on their way to Thebes. Creon he will not release until the old man brings the girls back. He condemns Creon's behavior but exempts the city of Thebes from his criticism: Theban training did not make him evil; that city does not breed lawless men and would not praise him for stealing his property and that of the gods.

The king's return carries something of the fragrance of melodrama.[28] Though nothing in the text suggests it, we could well imagine him riding in on a white horse. He forebears to unleash his righteous anger by physically harming the old man and will deal with him according to the law (905–8). His scrupulous treatment of Creon, combined with noble sentiments about Athenian reverence for justice, reaffirm his and Athens' position in the play as the extreme opposite of Creon and, despite Theseus's diplomatic distinction, Thebes. Both portraits seem exaggerated: if Theseus wears the white hat, Creon we may easily imagine twirling his mustache; he is, by any measure, a thoroughly nasty old man. Neither figure has anything like the depth and complexity of Oedipus. In this respect, it is useful to think of both as part of the spiritual geography we have seen Sophocles establishing: left, right; Thebes, Athens; past, present; black, white. Anchoring either end of this kind of schema does not require a subtly shaded character like Oedipus. He is destined for the Eumenides' grove, a site of unfathomable mystery identified with neither side, the gateway for Oedipus to transcendence of all mortal struggles.

Bolstered by Theseus's support, Oedipus launches a long rebuke to Creon, his final self-defense in the play. Calling him "shameless, arrogant" (*lēm' anaides*, 960), he once again denies any responsibility for the outcome of others' acts or of his own committed in ignorance. It is Creon who should be ashamed, for forcing him to talk about his incestuous marriage. He will now speak openly, since Creon has opened his "unholy mouth" (*anosion stoma*, 981). Creon has covered both Theseus and Athens with false flattery, as if that city did not know how to reverence the gods, while trying to snatch him and his daughters, an old man and his helpless children! He finishes with a prayer:

On account of these things, I call on these goddesses with
prayers of supplication to come to me as my helpers and allies,
that you may learn what kind of men guard this city!

(1010–13)

Creon continues to bluster ineffectually, but Theseus has matters in hand and forces him to lead the way to where he has Oedipus's daughters, leaving the stage to their father and the chorus.

In place of a messenger speech, what we might expect in response to events offstage, the chorus now sings its second stasimon, a rousing description of the battle the elders imagine to be taking place between the supporters of Athens and Thebes. The old men yearn to be where the armies wheel around to join the battle, to see Theseus victorious. They can picture the troops racing on horseback or in chariots:

Terrible the warcraft of the armies of Colonus,
terrible the strength of the sons of Thebes!

(1065–66)

They predict that the girls will be saved, calling on Zeus and Apollo to help their cause. The tone here fits with the melodrama preceding. The chorus' high-flown language seems excessive for portraying a minor border skirmish to prevent a sleazy kidnapping. In any event, being wholly imaginary, the song is not really commensurate with a messenger speech but is more akin in some ways to the "escape" lyrics that appear in later Euripides.[29] The focus is not so much on what Theseus and his troops are actually doing as on the fevered minds of the elders, carried away by their patriotic fervor.[30]

Happiness Postponed

As the chorus prophesied, Theseus now returns with Ismene and Antigone. An ecstatic reunion ensues. Oedipus issues a handsome speech of thanks to Theseus, praising him and Athens:

> Since I have received
> from you alone among mortals piety, fairness,
> and an aversion to speaking falsely.

> (1125–27)

So transported is Oedipus that he asks if he might touch Theseus's hand and kiss him, only to recoil in horror, remembering that he is not someone that the king could touch. This reminder of Oedipus's tainted nature throws into further relief his mysterious new power, his status as "sacred" (287). Theseus acknowledges this speech graciously, allowing that he needn't recount how he won the battle, since Ismene and Antigone will do so for him. But there is one thing: a man has arrived from Argos and sits as a suppliant beside the altar of Poseidon. He wishes to speak briefly to Oedipus.[31]

The gallant rescue and joyous reunion seem to form a natural conclusion to the narrative arc that begins with Oedipus arriving as stranger, seeking and winning protection from Athens and warding off abduction by the Thebans. He has now, it appears, triumphed over those who would drag him back to (or near) Thebes. We can imagine the play—now over twelve hundred lines—wrapping up soon, perhaps with that "consummation" that Oedipus has been promised. Instead, this intrusion into the family reunion jars, breaking the mood of relief and gratitude, creating an edgy atmosphere colored by Oedipus's abrupt refusal to see the stranger, who he is sure is his son, Polyneices. Though he may prefer to move on, Oedipus has one more piece of business to do with his past before he can turn toward the grove.[32]

Theseus urges him to reconsider, gently suggesting that since the man is a suppliant at Poseidon's altar, perhaps an audience would avoid angering the god. (And forbearing to draw the obvious parallel between Oedipus and his son as suppliants.) Antigone then takes up her brother's cause: why not honor Theseus's concern about the god and show mercy to his own son? She too suggests, ever so tactfully, that Oedipus might consider how unrestrained emotions have ruined his own earlier life: should he not restrain his anger and give Polyneices a hearing? Oedipus reluctantly agrees to let his son speak, but only if Theseus pledges not to let anyone "gain power over my life" (*mēdeis krateitō tēs emēs psuchēs*, 1207). The king agrees and exits to fetch the stranger.

Oedipus's anger at Polyneices is not surprising, given the latter's failure to help him when he faced exile. Still, we might expect that, having won his fight with Creon, he would now be disposed to show mercy to his own son. He has lived through a long struggle and presumably seen much of human frailty along the way. Why hang on to old grudges in the face of one's own death? But Oedipus has never been a gentle old man. He is meek and passive only when he lacks the power to exert his will. As we have now seen more than once, exposure to his Theban past animates him and brings out the pride and touchiness that marked his behavior as a young man there. Polyneices has stoked that flame, and though he will get a hearing, it will be a grudging one.

The chorus now sings its third stasimon in three parts, strophe, antistrophe, and epode (1211–48). The tone is subdued throughout, with the strophe focusing on death as the ultimate leveler:

> The same comrade comes for all alike,
> when Hades' destiny, without wedding songs,
> with no lyre and no dancing, appears,
> Death at the last.

> (1220–23)

The antistrophe turns to old age: powerless, friendless, and unloved, the last stage in a life that has seen murders, civil wars, quarrels, battles, and resentment. Better not to be born, with the next best being a quick death (1224–38). In the epode, the old men of the chorus identify with Oedipus, who is like a headland battered by storms of ruin from all sides (1239–48). If the reunion of father and daughters brought a wave of joy and relief, this song washes it away.

The picture of old age here is consistent with the usual dismal portrait found in Athenian tragedy.[33] The chorus' song echoes the dark cosmic view Polyneices has brought with him, so dominant in the Theban cycle of myths.

Tragedy in Miniature

Polyneices makes an unpromising start:

> Alas, what will I do? Shall I weep
> for my own evils, girls, or those of my father,
> which I see here? I find him thrown out
> in a strange land with you,
> wearing clothes like these; their ancient,
> ugly dirt has settled on my ancient father,
> rotting his flesh, and the uncombed hair
> on his sightless head flutters in the wind.
>
> (1254–61)

Though his distress may be genuine, these words sound rather like the insulting portrait of Oedipus that Creon offered earlier. The latter meant to shame Oedipus into coming with him. Polyneices seems more insensitive than malicious here, his own misery giving him something of a tin ear when it comes to the suffering of others. Though he does go on to admit that he has been a failure at supporting his father, he nonetheless expresses puzzlement at Oedipus's stubborn refusal to answer him. After Antigone declines to intervene, he tries again, opening by invoking the aid of Poseidon and Theseus, then passing on to describe his recent troubles:

> I have been driven from my fatherland, a fugitive,
> because having been born first, I thought myself
> worthy to sit on your throne, ruling over all.
> For this Eteocles, younger than I, drove
> me from my fatherland, not defeating me
> with words nor entering a contest of strength
> or action, but persuading the city. The reason for
> this, I think, is your Erinyes.
>
> (1292–99)

Again he fails to put his best foot forward, appearing initially not to notice that the wretched situation he finds himself in mirrors his father's plight as an exile, driven from Thebes while his sons did nothing.[34] Then almost as an aside, he blames all the trouble on Oedipus. The evil force of persuasion surfaces again, but in the present context it will be hard for Polyneices to make his brother the villain. Sweeping on, he describes each of the seven champions he has recruited to attack Thebes, the ornamental epithets and catalog style giving the passage an epic flavor. The elevated style here accompanies direct reference to the traditional myth that lies on the margins of our play, recalling the opening of *Electra*, where the Paedagogus's first speech invokes the mythical background for that play. In both works, the powerful portrait of an unconventional hero pushes the concerns of the myth to the margins of the drama. Polyneices finishes with a report on yet another oracle, this one saying that whichever son Oedipus favors will win the battle.

Some scholars have tried to make Polyneices a villain here, but he comes off as simply self-involved in a way typical of Greek heroes and consequently maladroit in his attempt to apologize to his father.[35] In any event, he would have to appear much more dastardly than he does to account for what comes next. Oedipus unleashes a horrendous tirade against both sons, blaming them for his exile, calling Polyneices *kakiste*, "the worst of men" (1354), who would have been the murderer of his own father had Antigone and Ismene not saved him. He declares that they are some other man's sons, not his, predicting that Polyneices will never destroy Thebes but die along with his brother. These are the curses he has pronounced on them in the past and he calls them forth again! If Zeus sits beside Justice, then his curses will vanquish all supplication and all mortal power. He rises to a hair-raising crescendo:

> Get out! I spit on you and am your father no more,
> most evil of evil men! Carry with you these curses
> I call down on you, so that you never conquer your homeland
> by spear nor ever return home to low-lying Argos, but
> die instead by your brother's hand and kill him who
> drove you out!
> These are my curses, and I call on the hateful
> fatherly gloom of Tartarus to give you a new home.
> I summon too these goddesses, and Ares,
> who has thrust this terrible hatred into your minds.

Hearing this, leave! Go tell all the Cadmeans
and your trusted allies, that Oedipus
has given prizes such as these to his own sons!

(1383–96)

Old age has not softened Oedipus's feelings about his sons, it would appear. Indeed, these lines reflect an increase in his anger. Perhaps this is not surprising, since in Polyneices he confronts a tie to his past that is intensely personal and intimate. That Oedipus resorts to curses is also unsurprising, as they are a source of power for old men in traditional societies. Being closer to death, the old man is thought to be closer to the gods and thus able to tap their power.[36] We may also see in Oedipus here some preview of the angry *daemōn* or supernatural spirit that Greeks believed to inhabit the graves of dead heroes, but to give this figure too much weight at this point would mask a crucial distinction. When he is dead, his power, however mysteriously, will flow from his status as a supernatural being. While he lives, the force of his curses—like the promise of his "gift" to Athens—is guaranteed by the gods, not by him. In this sense, Sophocles has created a hero whose power to influence people and events is not an aberrant form of the traditional model of the youthfully potent person but entirely characteristic of old men because of where they are in their lives. Sophocles presents, for the first and only time in tragedy, a paradigm for the aged hero.[37]

Equally important for our purposes is the way that Oedipus echoes the parallels that Polyneices has unwittingly cited between the two men's experience as exiles. Both are fugitives, driven out of their proper position in Thebes by those who should love and support them. It is as if Oedipus sees in Polyneices a version of his own younger self, which he then banishes to certain death. The intimacy of his connection to the dark power of Thebes is in this sense even greater than the link between father and son (a problematical enough relationship in the case of Oedipus and his children).[38] The curses he rains down on his sons recall the scourge of his own evil destiny or "Erinyes," as Polyneices calls it. As we will see, there is a kind of exorcism being performed here.

The chorus expresses sympathy for Polyneices and urges him to go back to Argos. He refuses, resigned now to his grim fate and determined to keep it a secret from his troops. He asks of his sisters that if Oedipus's curses come to fruition they give him a proper burial—producing a shiver in those who had seen *Antigone* thirty-five years before—for which they will gain more praise in addition to what they have won for looking after Oedipus. Antigone now tries to talk him out of proceeding to Thebes: he should take his army back to Argos. The exchange proceeds along lines familiar to Athenian theatergoers:

POLYNEICES
But that is impossible! For how could I
lead them back having once flinched in a crisis?

ANTIGONE
Why must you be angry again, brother, what
profit (*kerdos*) comes to you from ruining your country?

POLYNEICES
It is shameful to run away, and shameful to me,
the elder, to be mocked for it by my younger brother.

ANTIGONE
Do you see how you are carrying out this man's
prophecies, who foretold that you two would die at each other's hands?

POLYNEICES
He wants this, yes. Must we not comply?

ANTIGONE
Oh, I am wretched! Who would dare follow prophecies
Such as this man has uttered?

POLYNEICES
We will not report ugly news; it is right for
the commander to tell only better news, not what falls short.

(1418–30)

As Polyneices trudges off toward the left *eisodos* and Thebes, we are left to consider the meaning of what has just happened. It is not just that Oedipus has condemned his own sons, nor even that he has rejected Thebes and the version of himself that once lived there. Sophocles has gone to some trouble to bound off this episode, creating the expectation that the play was drawing to a close, then bringing on Polyneices with a new agenda and rounding it off with his exit.[39] The content itself contributes to our perception of the scene as a self-contained whole. As others have noted, what we witness here is an Athenian tragedy in miniature.[40] Polyneices, confronted with an inalterable necessity enforced by transcendent forces, elects to go to certain death rather than incur shame before his fellow warriors. Here is where the importance of his identification with the younger Theban Oedipus becomes clear: by rejecting Polyneices's plea for help and sending him to his death, Oedipus passes on to his son, as if it were a contagion, the tragic perspective that he himself held in his younger days, which has caused him and others so much misery.

In this scene, Sophocles has, then, staged a mini-tragedy for us. In doing so, he continues to use metatheatrical gestures, as he has in the previous two plays, to urge some detachment in the audience from the form itself. But now he takes a step further. In *Electra* and *Philoctetes*, characters on stage manipulate others by staging deceptive scenes, the Paedagogus playing the messenger for Clytemenestra, Neoptolemus and his sailors performing for Philoctetes. Here the recreation of a scene from tragedy is not part of a strategy by a character or characters to outwit anyone else on stage. Rather, the bounding-off and encapsulating of the exchange between Oedipus, Antigone, and Polyneices allows the playwright to portray his central character banishing entirely a vision of the world and the hero's place in it that has informed tragedy on the Athenian stage.[41] He is now ready to transcend the moral and ethical tangles that pervade traditional tragic stories and move to a mysterious vantage point wholly detached from them.

Into the Grove

Once Polyneices is offstage, the pace of events picks up. We are done with wrangling over Oedipus and the future site of his grave; forces tugging at the old man from the left and right disappear. The great consummation he has been promised is at hand, signaled by thunder and lightning from the gods. The chorus begins to sing anxiously, uncertain about whether the old man's prophecies will now come to fruition. They are answered at the end of a short strophe by the first crash of thunder: "The heavens have sounded, Oh Zeus" (1456). Oedipus, speaking in trimeters, immediately sends for Theseus, explaining to Antigone that the "winged thunder of Zeus" (1460) is calling him to Hades. Another crash of thunder punctuates the opening of the chorus' antistrophe. The elders are terrified by the celestial display, begging Zeus for mercy. Oedipus again announces the "prophesied end of his life" (1472–73). He brushes aside Antigone's doubts and calls a second time for someone to fetch Theseus. The chorus' fear and anxiety fill its second strophe, which begins after another peal of thunder and is followed by the third exchange in trimeters between Oedipus and Antigone, as Oedipus finally specifies for his daughter why he needs Theseus: in return for what Theseus and Athens have done for him, he wants to deliver the gift he promised (*telesphoron charin/dounai*, 1488–90). The chorus picks up again, calling now on Theseus to come and receive the gift.

Sophocles continues his flexible and inventive use of the chorus here. The high emotion prompted by the thunder—fear from the chorus, preemptive urgency in Oedipus—is articulated through a carefully balanced set of choral stanzas, punctuated by equally symmetrical exchanges between Oedipus and Antigone. The abrupt surge in dramatic energy is shaped by rhythmical symmetry and balance, as if to suggest that the seemingly chaotic forces of nature are themselves subject to the higher powers that will soon make their appearance.[42] Meanwhile, Theseus again races onstage, and again demands to know why he has been summoned. The echoes from his earlier arrival mark a parallel: once again he is entrusted with duties that no one else can fulfill (1500–07; 887–90).

Those duties he and we now learn from Oedipus. While the daughters may go partway to his final resting place in the grove, Theseus alone may accompany him to the actual spot for his grave. Proximity to it will give Athens protection forever. Theseus must not reveal this location to anyone else until he himself is near death. He should then pass on the knowledge only to the most eminent man, who in turn will guard the secret and pass it on when he dies.

We might well imagine that Oedipus has been sitting on the rock in the center of the orchestra for one thousand lines. He now rises to lead Theseus and his daughters through the central doors of the *skēnē* and into the grove beyond:

> Oh children, follow me. I am your new leader,
> as once you were for me.
> Come now, and do not touch me, but let me
> find the sacred tomb where I am
> destined to be hidden in this earth.
> This way, this way, come! For this way lead

Hermes the guide and the goddess of the Underworld.
O lightless light, you were mine before,
but now my body feels you for the last time.
For already I am going forth to hide in
Hades the end of my life. But come,
dearest of strangers, may you and your
attendants be blessed with good fortune,
and remember me for your unending success
when I am dead.

(1542–55)

Sophocles has been preparing for this procession since the opening scene of
this play, when we saw Oedipus tottering down the *eisodos* on the arm of Antigone. Frail there and utterly dependent on his daughter, he now leads everyone
toward the consummation of his extraordinary resurgence. The profound
change in him is marked by new perspectives on familiar themes: once the
thunder sounds, his view of time shifts, from unchanging cycles of suffering
and endurance to the urgency in finding *kairos*, the right time for action that
characterizes the masculine heroic persona of the other two plays (*hōs tachos*,
1461; cf. *El.* 1487ff.); appropriately suspicious of persuasive speakers earlier, he
persuades Theseus to follow his lead (*peitheis me*, 1516).[43]

With stage to themselves, the chorus sings a gentle prayer in two stanzas,
the first to Hades and Persephone, the second to Demeter, Persephone, and the
Eumenides. They ask that Oedipus, at the end of his many troubles, have a safe
journey to the underworld (1556–78). After this brief interlude comes a messenger from the grove to deliver the speech that the Athenian audience would
be expecting: Oedipus is dead; he "has left behind this ordinary life" (1583–84).
After he performed some ritual cleansing, thunder from Zeus prompted him to
summon his daughters to say goodbye. Tearful embraces were cut short by the
voice of a god, calling him often and from many places at once:

You there, Oedipus! Why do we delay
our departure? You have tarried for too long!

(1627–29)

Oedipus called for Theseus, forbade his daughters to go further with him, and
the two men disappeared into the grove. When those left behind turned to look

back, Oedipus was gone and Theseus was kneeling on the ground, shading his eyes as if from something *deinos*, which he could not bear to look at. The king then touched the ground and reached skyward, as if to salute both sources of divine power (1586–1666).

Antigone and Ismene return to the stage and sing, along with the chorus, a long *kommos*, a shared lament in strophic form (1670–1747). Mysterious as it was, the departure of Oedipus marked the end of his tumultuous life with a mood of tranquility and wholeness, symbolized in Theseus's final inclusive gesture to earth and sky. Now we return to the world of those he has left behind. Here there is only raw grief and anxiety for the future, as Sophocles creates his last complex lyrical ensemble. The girls exchange short phrases, often single words, with the chorus, feeding off each other's emotions, building to abject despair and helplessness:

> Alas, alas, where will we go, O Zeus?
> to what expectations is the god now
> driving us?
>
> (1748–50)

Theseus enters through the central doors and commands the daughters to cease their laments. Mourning is not appropriate for someone who goes to the underworld by the grace of the gods. We are familiar by now with the rhythm of this passage, mounting emotion and disorder quelled by the arrival of the masterful king. But this time Theseus cannot deliver relief. The girls ask to see their father's tomb, but he refuses. The gift Oedipus has promised depends on Theseus keeping his secret. Antigone acquiesces in her father's final command, heading off the left *eisodos*, toward Thebes and the miserable future that all in the audience know is coming for her and Ismene. Even though they were faithful helpmates for their father, they will be destroyed by the same tragic milieu as their brothers. Oedipus has passed into a new existence, but tragedy remains.[44]

Conclusion: Into Mystery

Oedipus at Colonus is the second-longest extant Athenian tragedy. Its episodic structure and melodramatic passages have not always pleased critics,[45] but the articulation of the plot is always in the service of Sophocles's thematic purposes. Indeed, making us wait sometimes serves those purposes: he keeps us engaged by *not* fulfilling our expectations. We are looking eagerly for Theseus when Ismene arrives; Polyneices, having spoiled the celebration after Creon is defeated, then prolongs the play for almost two hundred lines as we await the great consummation promised in the opening scene.[46] This last episode is in turn crucial for our understanding of how Sophocles pushes his paradigm for the hero's life—with which he has already been exploring new territory in the previous two plays—to a new level of meaning in his last work.

Despite the many parallels between the old Oedipus and his heroic predecessors in *Electra* and *Philoctetes*, the story of the old man's last day stands apart from the previous two works—and indeed most of Greek tragic literature—in its insistence on the need to *transcend* the tensions and struggles, the *agōnes*, that dominate so much of ancient Greek culture.[47] And this aspect of Sophocles's last play is most evident in the placement and function of the Polyneices episode. By passing on his tragic curse to his son, who then carries it back to Thebes, its natural home, Oedipus prepares not to affirm his choice of Athens over Thebes but to move beyond that contest to another plane of existence. Thus the clever tongue (802) of Creon is finally less important than his connection to Oedipus's doomed past; his principal tools are in fact bullying and shaming, part of the traditional heroic perspective, not tricky speaking. Polyneices resembles not Odysseus but Neoptolemus, a would-be tragic hero who is if anything too straightforward in speech. That he is dispatched just prior to the gods calling Oedipus to his destiny affirms his role as carrier of the self-destructive persona of tragic hero.

Oedipus's new persona, the principal vehicle in the play for the movement toward transcendence, can be best understood through the function of gifts in the play. Defending himself against the old charges, Oedipus pleads that Jocasta was a "gift" (*dōron*, 540) to him that he should never have accepted. Later, he pledges to Theseus his own wretched body as a gift, *dōsōn hikanō toumon athlion demas* (576). Greek marriage practices would suggest that Jocasta was given as a body to be used, and, as we discover, Oedipus thinks of himself in a similar way. His ruined body can be used by the Athenians after he is dead. Proximity to his physical remains will bring power to his adopted city, especially in their struggles with Thebes. Oedipus speaks twice of the "profit" his corpse can bring to Athens (92, 288), again focusing on his physical being as object.

To those he would help, the hero usually offers himself as an active agent, perhaps using his body but always directing it by the exercise of his own will.

The old Oedipus's body will also help others, but *he* will not use it to do so. The gods will use his body as the conduit for *their* power. Now instead of reciprocal, two-way giving, we have an expanded circle of givers and those who receive. Those who give are not to expect an immediate return from the ones to whom their gift passes. Rather, they must give and watch their gift pass out of their sight, trusting that it will circle back to them some other time from a place they cannot now see.

Lewis Hyde, in exploring the implications of such a "gift economy," contrasts its operation and underlying assumptions to a market economy:

> It is this element of relationship which leads me to speak of gift exchange as an "erotic" commerce, opposing *eros* (the principle of attraction, union, involvement which binds together) to *logos* (reason and logic in general, the principle of differentiation in particular). A market economy is an emanation of *logos*.[48]

Central to understanding how such a system works is the distinction Hyde draws between "profit" and "increase:"

> The increase begins when the gift has passed *through* someone, when the circle appears. But . . . "profit" is not the right word. Capital earns profit and the sale of a commodity turns a profit, but gifts that remain gifts do not *earn* profit, they give increase. The distinction lies in what we might call the vector of increase: in gift exchange it, the increase, stays in motion and follows the object, while in commodity exchange it stays behind as profit.[49]

The "profit" (*kerdos, onēsis*) that Oedipus offers to the Athenians through the gift of his body is a part of Hyde's "erotic commerce." It will bind Oedipus, Athens, and the gods, bringing increase, not the residual profit of the market economy.[50]

Because gifts that move in this way affirm connection, not the separation that a hero's extraordinary abilities usually enforce, the pledge Oedipus makes to Athens is unique in Athenian tragedy. The fragile relationship between the hero and his or her community is always at the heart of Sophocles's tragic stories. If the hero's will is trained on goals that serve the community, much good can come from the relationship. But heroic will and communal well-being rarely coincide indefinitely, and once they diverge, only pain, for both sides, can ensue. In his earlier Oedipus play, Sophocles presents a particularly subtle exploration of this dynamic. The young Oedipus believes that he is serving the well-being of Thebes by pursuing, with all the force of his heroic will, the murderer of Laius. Once he succeeds, he destroys himself and also his community, which depends on its king to be its intermediary with the gods.

By expanding the relationship between Oedipus and Athens to include the gods, Sophocles obviates the usual clash between individual heroic will and the good of the community. Now Oedipus can serve his adopted home, but not through the expression of his own will. Rather, he will participate in a gift circle, in which he becomes a channel for the expression of divine will. And because the gods are part of the process, the struggles that dominate the earlier scenes of the play are made to seem small, as if seen through the wrong end of a telescope. Indeed, it may well be that the melodramatic aspects of the play—Theseus's dismissive impatience with the arguing of Creon and Oedipus; the exaggerated black-and-white coloring of Creon and Theseus; the chorus' overblown imagining of the border skirmish—are part of the playwright's larger purpose. All of this intrigue, pain, and willful self-destructiveness recedes from the foreground, now taken up with Oedipus's mysterious communion with the gods.

The old Oedipus stands apart from all other Sophoclean tragic heroes because finally he does not understand the meaning of his life *as against* the operation of larger, often mysterious forces in the universe. Rather, he is important precisely because he fits into a larger plan, much of which he can never understand, none of which is under the control of his will. That he simply disappears, gathered into the company of the gods, is an appropriate ending for his life as he comes to understand it on the last day of his life.

But startling as this new vision is, *Oedipus at Colonus* shares with every other example of Sophocles's tragic art the insistent focus on what it means to be human. Though Oedipus breaks new ground because he achieves a level of transcendence, he and we always view the prospect the gods have spread before him from the perspective of a limited, mortal life. What does it mean, how does it inform the meaning of a human life, we are invited to ask, to be a person whom the gods have chosen to be the vehicle for carrying out their mysterious purposes?[51]

CHAPTER 5

Late Sophocles

The last ten years of Sophocles's life must have been an anxious time in Athens. Crushing the Melians, sailing for Sicily only to starve in the stone quarries, the Athenian navy displays the imperialist politics of the city hardening after the temporary respite of the Peace of Nicias. Thucydides shines a harsh light on both episodes, with their debased rhetoric and misplaced optimism.[1] In 413 BCE, as hopes wane in Sicily, Sparta invades Attica for the first time in several years and builds a permanent fort in Decelea, a few miles north of the city. Farmers crowd back inside the walls from the countryside, returning the city to the overcrowded conditions that fueled the plague of 430–29. The oligarchs seize control in 411; democracy is restored in 410, but not without casualties. By the time Sophocles dies in 406, with the losses in Sicily and elsewhere draining the city's treasury, the city's leaders are melting temple treasures and debasing the coinage. Victory at Arginusae in 406 offers some hope, but the victorious commanders fail to save two thousand sailors in the aftermath and are killed for their efforts. Still, victory might have allowed the Athenians to arrange a favorable peace, but they press on to ultimate defeat in 404.

In this edgy atmosphere, Sophocles created his last three plays. What must he have been thinking about his city and its prospects? We have only the late plays to go on, and reading them as a mirror of contemporary events has proved a difficult project for Classical scholars.[2] Yet it seems inconceivable that these works did not reflect the strains of a turbulent time. What little we do know about his life puts Sophocles squarely in the middle of the affairs of his city, as priest, general, councilor, but especially as playwright. His medium as an artist, tragic drama, was central to the civic and religious life of Athens to a degree perhaps never again seen in the Western world.³ In the Theater of Dionysus, Athenians could see enacted, over and over, the myths that addressed critical issues in their lives.

It is easy to see how the pressures of a long war energized certain old stories. Euripides's *Trojan Women* and Aristophanes's *Lysistrata* reflect in their different ways the suffering of women during wartime, a central theme in both Homeric epics; the former's *Electra* and two *Iphigenia* plays focus on a daughter sacrificed to male aggression. At the same time, the intellectual ferment of the fifth century, bubbling up alongside the new democratic form of government, had produced debates about the nature of human life, the role of the gods in human affairs, the best form of society, which seem to have penetrated the political arena in ways that made some—including Sophocles—thoughtful if not uneasy. Thucydides's harrowing account of the Melian dialogue shows political rhetoric in Athens deteriorating under the pressures of war. Through his eyes we see the Sicilian Expedition as an example of the dangerously seductive operation of persuasion in the Athenian assembly. The Sophists have left their mark on the narration of both episodes.⁴

The Hero in Place

Summarizing the various innovations we find in Sophocles's dramatic practice in the late plays is challenging, but one recurrent set of preoccupations centers on the *position* of the hero, understood on various levels. On the one hand, each of Sophocles's last three heroes lacks to some degree typical heroic agency, the ability to impress his or her will out onto the world through his or her body. This deficit was usually understood by the Greeks to be gendered: the willful thrust of energy and desire to control was seen as a masculine trait. This is not to say that female characters in Greek literature do not sometimes show masculine traits (see Aeschylus's Clytemnestra and Euripides's Medea). But Electra, though fierce in her determination not to accept her father's murder, is presented as without direct agency in the play. Philoctetes, because of his lack of mobility, his oozing, smelly wound (reminiscent of the odiferous women of Lemnos), his experience of time as something to be endured rather than seized, is feminized, a victim of male conspirators. Oedipus is akin to the Teiresias of *Oedipus Tyrannus*, who is said to "nourish" (*trephō*) power within himself, a kind of midwife (Soph. *OT* 356). All three heroes have bodies characterized by inwardness, latency, which the Greeks associated with women and things feminine; all three are used in one way or another by males who want to manipulate them for their own ends.

These distinctions between the hero and his or her tormentors are aligned in the late plays with the intellectually potent polarity of *logos/ergon*. Orestes, his Paedagogus, Pylades, Odysseus, Neoptolemus, his sailors, Creon and Polyneices, all are agents of *logos*. All hope to use words, usually deceptive ones, to control the stubborn hero, whose body finally represents the unwieldy and inconvenient *ergon*. Certain polarities begin to emerge: shifty, deceptive words versus suffering bodies; active manipulation versus passive endurance; sophistic rhetoric versus traditional aristocratic values; appearance versus reality. Echoes of the intellectual debates in fifth-century Athens are clear enough, with the plays seeming to valorize a somewhat more conservative, aristocratic perspective.[5] The imperialist excesses of the period also find analogues here, often launched from an assembly fired by overreaching rhetoric.

At the same time, heroic bodies as physical objects (as opposed to subjects) on stage influence the outcome of all three plays. The male conspirators in *Electra* twice pretend to present the corpse of Orestes, whom we might expect to be the hero, inside the urn as ashes and on the *ekkyklēma* in the final scene. These deceptions forward the plan to murder the royal couple precisely because in each case the remains are *not* Orestes. But encountering the real body of his sister, wasted by anger and deprivation, suddenly shocks Orestes into recognizing Electra's genuine suffering as a result of the family's horrors. At that moment, Sophocles's dramatic purposes become particularly clear: his play is centered not on the avenging son's return but on the ruined daughter, imprisoned by her mother and stepfather. To put it another way, the play reflects the impact of war and its aftermath on the women who stay at home while their male relatives pursue power over others. If we are looking for evidence that Sophoclean drama was shaped by contemporary events, this might be a place to begin.[6]

Philoctetes is defined from the beginning by his body: marooned on Lesbos, prevented from exerting heroic force, repellent to others because of his wound.[7] He smells bad and makes too much noise. In the opening scene, the sailors cower in anticipation of his arrival, imagining him as a primeval creature, barely human. His salvation begins when he recreates himself before Neoptolemus and the sailors as a part of heroic culture instead of a liminal curiosity of nature: a Greek warrior, friend of Achilles and Ajax, bitter enemy of Agamemnon and Menelaus. But as he distances himself from the Polyphemus paradigm in the eyes of Neoptolemus, the demands of the oracle—which are the demands of the myth—focus our attention on his body. Despite some initial ambiguity, it emerges in the course of the play that the fall of Troy requires that Philoctetes's body be present there.

The pivotal moment comes in *Philoctetes*, as it does in *Electra*, when one of the male plotters has an intense encounter with the hero's body. Philoctetes falls to the ground, rendered unconscious by the pain in his wounded foot. Neoptolemus, though he has been showing signs of weakening resolve, has managed to keep pressing forward with the plot to deceive Philoctetes and get the bow to Troy. Seeing his new friend in a deathlike state jolts the young man and he is unable to keep on deceiving Philoctetes. In terms of Neoptolemus's education, this is the moment when he chooses once and for all to honor his father Achilles's genetic inheritance rather that the sophistic program of Odysseus. He continues to try to convince Philoctetes to sail with him to Troy, but he will not lie anymore.

Sophocles's last play is articulated primarily through the lateral movement, symbolic and actual, of the hero's body across the stage.[8] Blind and feeble, Oedipus is pulled now toward Thebes, now Athens, and finally walks under his own power into the grove of the Eumenides. The events from this part of the Theban cycle of myths, though kept at a distance during the action, all depend on his final place of rest. Sophocles pushes his new paradigm for the tragic hero even further here than in the disabled figure of Philoctetes, who must be moved to Troy but once there is destined to shoot the fatal arrow himself. Oedipus is entirely without physical agency until his last moments on earth. His body, as he tells Theseus, is to be a gift for Athens, but one which the city can only receive after he is dead and buried. Though while alive he is characteristically willful in the way of Sophoclean heroes, the power of his gift comes from the gods and finally will pass through him without the direct operation of his will.

The position of the bodies of these late heroes, onstage and off, is crucial, then, to the leverage that each exerts in his or her story. We may extend this idea of positioning to the placement within the narrative of each figure in relation to the traditional myth that informs the plot. In all three late plays, Sophocles offers us an oblique perspective on traditional myths. I mean the term "oblique" in a fairly literal sense: our line of sight is displaced. Attention is focused on Electra, Philoctetes, and the aged Oedipus, nothing unusual about that. But as we have seen, each of these figures, whose points of view inform our understanding of the action, is detached in some way from the main thrust of the narrative that carries the traditional myth. Orestes and the Paedagogus move purposefully toward the goals of the myth—in this case the murders of Clytemnestra and Aegisthus—while Electra, on whom Sophocles has trained our attention, stands apart and reacts to events. She embodies and is defined by the familiar heroic struggle against forces beyond her control. Her inner darkness, swirling with resentment and self-hatred, contrasts strongly with the opportunism of Orestes and the Paedagogus, colorless men of action too shallow to carry the weight of the Sophoclean hero's burden.

We see Philoctetes at first through the eyes of the conspirators, Odysseus, Neoptolemus, and the chorus, a lonely cave creature beyond the pale of human civilization, an object of anxious fascination for those who would trap him. As he gradually comes into sharper focus through exchanges with Neoptolemus and the chorus, Philoctetes moves from outsider to insider, establishing himself as a fellow Greek warrior betrayed by his commanders. The conspirators work on him with lies and playacting, trying to align his desires with the demands of the oracles that define the goals of the myth, here the destined fall of Troy. Again, he fits the heroic profile in terms of temperament, while his pursuers remain the agents of the myth on stage.

The separation of heroic temper and mythical plot is more complex here than in *Electra*. Neoptolemus, though somewhat naïve, is by genetic inheritance and—as it eventually turns out—temperament, heroic material. His education, handled by Odysseus and then Philoctetes, seems to point to him as potentially the play's hero. But as Philoctetes's stubbornness and self-destructive tendencies come out, he displaces the young man as the focus of the play. His continued refusal to bend before the imperatives of the myth keeps him detached from the plotters' perspective and holds the mythical story at a distance, far off at Troy.

Oedipus at Colonus leaves the site of its traditional myth offstage in Thebes. The old Oedipus spends much of his time fending off both the consequences of his past acts there and the forces that would pull him toward the dismal future that awaits his children. His late scene with Polyneices seems designed specifically to allow him to separate himself from the Theban cycle of myths. Polyneices, as he trudges to Thebes and certain death, carries with him the Erinyes of his father. Once he is gone, Oedipus moves toward the site of his eventual transcendence of all human life.

A New World

Whatever his reservations in old age about the message or medium of his art, the power of Sophocles's last works is undeniable. And finally, we have only the work. Knowing more about Sophocles's life outside of his plays might tempt us to speculate about the connections between his biography and his art, the way scholars like to think about the reflection in his late quartets of Beethoven's loneliness or hearing loss. Maybe it is just as well that we are spared those alluring possibilities. We can on the other hand be reasonably sure that *Philoctetes* and *Oedipus at Colonus* are products of the last five years of his extraordinarily long life, with *Electra* likely coming shortly before. These works comprise Sophocles's "late work," and as such they might invite comparison to the final creations of other famous artists, such as Rembrandt, Shakespeare, or Beethoven.

The whole subject of "last works" and/or "late style" has come under scrutiny recently, and some distinctions have emerged that will be useful here.[9] First of all, the artist whose work spans a long period might be expected to have learned his or her craft, to have solved or at least worked through artistic problems that caused trouble in earlier years. Living to a ripe age would at least offer the opportunity for growth. Of course, there is no guarantee that lessons will be learned. Bad art can persist. And some artists—Mozart being an obvious example—start making extraordinary work early, so a shorter life might not rule out this kind of seasoning. Apart from the ripening of skills, there is the question of the artist's perspective as it might reflect his or her time of life. The awareness of mortality weighs on anyone who feels it close, and the older an artist gets, the more likely that death's nearness will be felt. Thus we may want to proceed cautiously in appraising Mozart's "late" works. We might be tempted to see his *Requiem* as composed in the shadow of his own death, but nothing else in his last year suggests that he felt he was composing his final works.[10]

Edward Said, writing at the end of his own life, added another *caveat*. Commenting on the frequent image of the artist in old age who has achieved a certain serenity and detachment from the struggles that mark earlier stages in life, he suggests an alternative version:

> Each of us can readily supply evidence of how it is that late works crown a lifetime of aesthetic endeavor, Rembrandt and Matisse, Bach and Wagner. But what of artistic lateness not as harmony and resolution but as intransigence,

difficulty, and unresolved contradiction? What if old age and ill health don't produce the serenity of "ripeness is all"?[11]

Much has been written about *The Tempest* as an example of the former paradigm, though not every Shakespearean would agree.[12] Examples of the latter would likely include Beethoven and Ibsen.[13] Rembrandt's last portraits (and self-portraits) certainly project a detachment from immediate time and place, but whether they project serenity is another thing. The weathered face we see might just as well reflect anguish and struggle as serenity.

About Sophocles's technical mastery of his craft in the last three plays there is no doubt. His handling of the chorus in particular shows considerable innovation. Otherwise, the late work lies somewhat athwart these distinctions. We would hardly be tempted to call any of the plays "autumnal" or "serene," though at the end of *Oedipus at Colonus* the old hero steps calmly into timelessness. Nor, on the other hand, would we say that any of the plays goes "against the grain," in terms of the standard forms associated with tragedy, though the playwright uses familiar elements to achieve a radical reimagining of the genre's central figure. The final trio of works might best be understood as combining retrospection with innovation. On the one hand, each of the plays looks back to significant themes and characters from earlier in the performance history of tragedy or, in the case of *Philoctetes*, from Homeric epic. Sophocles revives the Orestes cycle of myths, which had appeared in the *Oresteia* almost fifty years before. *Philoctetes* becomes an extended negotiation between the legacies of Achilles and Odysseus, with a brief but crucial cameo from Polyphemus. In the last play, Sophocles's most famous creation returns for an extraordinary farewell.

Yet while the playwright looks back to gather up familiar material, it is always in the service of a fresh perspective. Many new ways of thinking and seeing pervade Sophocles's last plays, but our understanding of them must begin with his hero, the arresting figure he did so much to create over his long career. When we say that the heroes of his late plays depart from what we have come to expect, the standard against which we measure them derives primarily from his own earlier works.[14] There, more than in Aeschylus or Euripides, the lonely hero demands our attention. Not as someone to admire, but as a lightning rod, who draws the powers of the universe to him/herself, who stands on—or more likely crosses—the boundaries that the Greeks understood as shaping the cosmos. Sophocles offers us multiple perspectives on the action and speech of the characters, but finally we see everything through the lens of the hero. So when he reimagines that figure, our view of everything on stage and beyond changes.

One effect of showing the action slantwise in the last three plays is to shine a light on the suffering of those who are not in the chain of command, abused women, wounded soldiers, old men cast out of their homes. The scope widens in *Philoctetes*, showing the hero, who recalls Electra in many ways, against a backdrop of expanded causation, in which his will, while still formidable, does not drive the action that the myth's outcome requires. The familiar dynamic of tragic narratives, a hero's will opposed to transcendent forces, becomes more complex here. We see Philoctetes first as part of a larger plan, reflecting the mysterious purposes of the gods. He must eventually act, but only if and when he and his bow are moved by others to Troy. His opposition to divine will, the emblem of the tragic hero, only emerges around line 900, after he learns of the conspirators' deception. Once his own fierce defiance comes into view, he, and not Neoptolemus, emerges fully as the hero of the play. At that point we may in turn begin to recognize the pattern of displacement we saw first in *Electra*, underscored by the similarities between that play's hero and Philoctetes.

The compressed portrait of Philoctetes as hero may help to explain Sophocles's use of the deus ex machina, an unusual move for him as far as we can tell. Because we have been invited from the play's opening scenes to understand Philoctetes's importance in the context of larger forces, their return in the person of Herakles is not as jarring as it might be. In any event, by having the god impose the proper ending, the playwright preserves his hero's heroic temperament without having him destroyed in the process. He remains a Sophoclean hero but his agency can be folded into the gods' larger purposes nonetheless.

The implications of this shift of perspective come to full flower in *Oedipus at Colonus*. Whereas Philoctetes retains his characteristic defiance of larger forces even as he becomes an instrument of them, Oedipus walks on stage determined to follow the will of the gods. He will seek death not as the only alternative to capitulation but as the glorious consummation of his long life. Willful he can be, but his defiance is of those who would keep him from obeying, not resisting, divine will. His mysterious redemption is all about finding a way to fit himself into the larger rhythms of the universe. In so doing, Sophocles's last hero steps outside the arena where so much of Greek tragic literature, beginning with the *Iliad*, is played out. The characteristic struggle between the hero's will, which s/he sees as the engine of self-creation, and the often mysterious imperatives of larger forces, does not appear in *Oedipus at Colonus*. For Achilles, for the younger Oedipus, for Ajax, Electra, Antigone, and surely many other Sophoclean heroes in plays now lost to us, impressing his or her will on other people and things is the path to self-realization. To put it another way, to get one's way is to become oneself.

And the world onstage is formed by this vision. Heroes make things happen by working their will on people and things around them. Others do what they can in the wake of these powerful figures and we look on at the world this dynamic creates. So when the old Oedipus walks into the grove, drawing the power of the gods through himself as he is being drawn toward them, he leaves us a different world, one in which we can find fulfillment by playing our part in a larger field of forces, whose powers are not ours to direct. The result of this final consummation is difficult to fix in words, because we are so conditioned by the Western view of consciousness that valorizes individual will. To understand one's life as part of a larger circle of gifts is challenging, but this view is surely what Sophocles dramatizes in his last play.

Notes

Preface

1. All translations of Greek are mine.
2. See Jacobsen 1976; Van Nortwick 1992, 8–38.
3. Taplin 1977 and 1978.
4. E.g., Seale 1982; Padel 1990; Rehm 1992 and 2002; Edmunds 1996; Wiles 1997; Ringer 1998. For a thoughtful discussion of the challenges facing a director of ancient drama on a modern stage, see Gamel 2002.
5. Anyone who studies the meters of Greek tragedy has reason to be grateful for the work of A.M. Dale (1968; 1971; 1981).
6. E.g., Burton 1980; Scott 1996. See also Kitzinger's study of Sophocles's *Antigone* and *Philoctetes*, a challenging vision of the chorus's unique presence on stage.
7. Reinhardt 1979; Whitman 1951; Knox 1964; Segal 1981.

Chapter 1

1. On the dating of *Electra*, see Whitman 1951, 51–54; March 2001, 20–22; Lloyd 2005, 16–18; Finglass 2007, 1–4; Ferrario 2012, 456. Reinhardt 1979, 135–38 makes a strong case for grouping *Electra* with the last two plays.
2. See Ringer 1998, 92, who says that Sophocles's unusually complex doubling and tripling of roles in *Oedipus at Colonus* "sustains Sophocles' extraordinarily fluid dramatic structure and stands testimony to the versatility of late fifth-century actors, as well as to the innovative courage of the octogenarian playwright." And further, of the virtuosity of Sophocles as a playwright and the virtuosity he demands of his cast in the last play: "They also reveal a playwright capable of great technical daring, even at the end of an unusually long and successful career" (93).
3. On Sophocles and Homer, see now Schein 2012, with bibliography.

4. See Van Nortwick 2012.

5. See Ringer 1998. Hall 2009, 105–11, notes that the term "metatheater" refers to several types of representation onstage. She objects to the use of the phrase "play-within-a-play" when referring to Greek drama, which she says has no examples of characters explicitly creating dramas within dramas. What I call "play-within-a-play" she would identify as "role-playing within a role." I see her point, but for the purposes of this discussion, I will use "putting on a scene" or "play-within-a-play" to refer to any scene in the plays I discuss that features a character or characters pretending to be someone else for the purpose of deceiving other characters. See further Inoue 2009, 48–49.

6. Guthrie 1971, 250–60. For a thorough overview of the intellectual context in fifth-century Athens for the plays, see Goldhill 1986, *passim* and especially 222–43.

7. On the "performative" aspects of Athenian culture, see Rehm 1992, 3–11.

8. *Il.* 11. 654; 19. 17.

9. Knox 1964, chaps. 1–2; see especially 44. See also Winnington-Ingram 1980, 9, 317; Lloyd 2005, 78–79. Finglass 2011, 42–44, voices reservations about the phrase "Sophoclean hero" used to describe the protagonists of Sophocles's plays. He takes issue with those who see no criticism, explicit or implicit, of the behavior and character of heroes in Sophocles's plays, arguing that these scholars are confusing the function of the protagonist with the term "hero," which, he says, "implies moral approval" (43). I would certainly agree that the heroes of Sophocles's plays are not presented by the playwright in such a way as to imply unequivocal moral approval. This understanding of the word "hero" is anachronistic, importing modern notions of "heroism" into Archaic Greek culture. Greek heroes are characterized by arrogance, excess, and intransigence in the face of uncontrollable forces, hardly the qualities that insure moral approval.

10. See Dunn 2012, especially 99–100, 103.

11. Scodel 2012 gives a thorough survey. See also Lloyd 2005, 14–16; Kelly 2009, 9–14.

Chapter 2

1. For Homeric references in this description, see Finglass 2007, 92–101.

2. For an excellent discussion of this scene, see Kitzinger 1991, 302–5.

3. On *kairos* in Greek drama, see Race 1981, 210–11.

4. Stanford 1968, 102–7. See Seale 1982, 56–57, on the visual impact of the scene and on the ironic disparity between heroic language and an unheroic plan.

5. For a discussion of the opposition in fifth-century thought, see Parry 1981, 16–62. See also Wilson 2012, 548–50. Woodard 1964 pursues the polarity as it informs the dialectic he sees represented in the characters of Orestes and Electra. He argues (164–65) that the use of *kairos*, *ergon*, and *kerdos* in the opening scene suggests the presence of "mercantile ethics," a perspective at odds, one would think, with the aristocratic tone of Orestes's opening remarks, thus undermining his heroic profile.

6. See Guthrie 1971, 250–60; Goldhill 1986, 222–43.

7. See Parry 1981, 47–51.

8. Segal 1981, 250, 257, casts the contrast between the worlds of Electra and Orestes in terms of "inner" and "outer," a formulation that fits the imagery of much of the play. At the same time, since Electra is on stage for the entire play, outside the palace, while Orestes disappears for long stretches, Segal's polarity might be seen as reversed as the action unfolds. And at the end, Orestes and Aegisthus go into the dark palace, while Electra remains outside.

9. On the different ways of experiencing time in the play, see Segal 1981, 262–67; see especially 265, on the gendered relationship between *kairos* and circular time.

10. Since Electra reminds us that Procne actually killed the son she mourns to retaliate against her husband, who had raped her sister Philomela, the mythical paradigm adds a further shade of darkness to the portrait—perhaps some acknowledgment of her own part in her childlessness? See Segal 1981, 256–57.

11. See further Finglass 2007, 132.

12. For Oedipus as an Erinys in *Oedipus at Colonus,* see Gellie 1972, 168.

13. Goldhill 2012, 113–19, has an excellent discussion of the innovations in the *parodos.*

14. See further Burton 1980, 188–90.

15. See Seale 1982, 59. Kitzinger 1991, 306–7, sees Electra as the "victor" over the chorus in this exchange. Though Electra does elicit a promise of support from the women (251–53), her tone is not, to my ears, victorious so much as lonely and resigned (see 254–55).

16. See Reinhardt 1979, 136–38.

17. Whether this play was produced before or after Euripides's *Electra* is an ongoing question, for which the surviving evidence will not provide a definitive answer. I incline to an earlier date for Sophocles's version, but even if Euripides's play was produced first, the Electra in his play, while certainly powerful and disturbing, hardly qualifies as a heroic figure. See Whitman 1951, 51–54; Gellie 1972, 119, n. 15; Lloyd 2005, 17–18, 31–32; and Finglass 2007, 1–4, all with bibliography.

18. On Orestes as "untragic," see Reinhardt 1979, 137. On Electra as heroic vs. Orestes, Segal 1966, 511: "What is truly heroic in the play, then, rests with Electra. She, rather than Orestes, has been able to win her way, in a debased world, to a living sense of past greatness. She is the one who defends the bonds of *physis* most vigorously." Kitto 1950, 133, seems to suggest that both Orestes and Electra are heroes in the play, though without much explanation. See also Whitman 1951, 154–55; Woodard 1964, 166–67; Blundell 1989, 173–74; Foley 2001, 158–59.

19. See Gellie 1972, 106.

20. Whitman 1951 sees Sophocles's last period, encompassing the final three plays, as "purgatorial," in that "it deals with the soul's use of time" (150–51). For him, the heroes of those plays exemplify a "new kind of arete, the arete of Odysseus . . . embracing the

qualities of endurance, courage, skill, and self-control" (151). This seems a good description of the Homeric Odysseus but not the figure we often encounter in Athenian tragedy. Electra as we find her in this play actually projects an Odyssean capacity for endurance in the service of an Achillean intransigence. See also Woodard 1964, 206.

21. Van Nortwick 2009, 105–10.

22. See Gellie 1972, 108; Segal 1981, 254; Seale 1982, 79–80.

23. Woodard 1964 suggests that Sophocles means us to see Orestes and Electra as together forming "a paradigm of the fully heroic, of full human excellence" (170). His dialectical model for the play, while identifying important elements of the characterization of both principals, seems unlikely to have worked dramatically on stage. On the polarities represented by the two characters, see further the exhaustive discussion in Segal 1981, 249–91.

24. For the differences between the two scenes, see Whitman 1951, 157. On the exchange between Electra and Chrysothemis, see Blundell 1989, 157–61.

25. See Kitzinger 1991, 308.

26. On Electra's "moral absolutism," see Woodard 1964, 168–69.

27. See Segal 1966, 532, on the *logos/ergon* polarity in the relationship of Electra and Orestes.

28. Foley 2001, 151–59, analyzes Electra's position as an example of the "ethics of vendetta," wherein lament functions as something like *ergon*. See also Seale 1982, 75: "It is [Electra's] play and this horror is her affair, expressed in the peculiar logic of the play whereby the passive power of emotion becomes by its very explicitness a kind of action." For the Homeric view of words as deeds, see further Parry 1981, 21–22; for Electra's words as deeds, Blundell 1989, 157; on Electra's view, see further Ormand 1999, 61.

29. Hutchinson 1999, 51–58.

30. See Carson 1990, 143: "The unfailing moisture and sexual drive of women is part of a larger pattern, part of a larger harmony between women and the elements of nature in general. United by a vital liquidity with the elemental world, woman is able to tap the inexhaustible reservoirs of nature's procreative power. Man, meanwhile, holds himself fiercely and thoughtfully apart from this world of plants, animals, and female wantonness—doubly estranged from it, by his inherent dryness and by the *sophrosyne* with which he maintains form."

31. On Electra and Clytemnestra, see Whitman 1951, 157–58; Segal 1966, 501; Gellie 1972, 114–15; Segal 1981, 260–62; Griffiths 2012, 76–77.

32. See Ormand 1999, 64–65 and Segal 1981, 261.

33. On this exchange, see Winnington-Ingram 1980, 219–24, who reads the play as a response to the Aeschylean disposal of the moral conflict; also Segal 1966, 476; Blundell 1989, 150–53, 161–72; Lloyd 2005, 85–90.

34. On the moral issues raised by the matricide see further Segal 1966, 540: ". . . its [the play's] 'success' does not lie in solving the moral problems of the Orestes legend. These problems do not lie at the center of the play, but do contribute to the tone of ir-

resolution and the continued presence of 'evils' in the end (see 1498)." For a complementary view, see Kitzinger 1991, 311–12. See also Whitman 1951, 159–60; Dunn 2012, 97–101. On the mythological background for Sophocles's treatment of matricide, see Lloyd 2005, 19–31; Griffiths 2012, 74–76. About moral conflict in Greek tragedy more generally, see also the useful remarks of Blundell 1989, 11–12.

35. On Electra's character here, see Kirkwood 1958, 140; Scodel 1984, 86; Segal 1981, 251; Seaford 1985; Kitzinger 1991, 316–17. The interplay of voices in the scene between Electra and Clytemnestra seems to me to offer evidence that Athenian drama could portray psychological states effectively, *pace* Rehm 1992, 38. See, on the other hand, his insightful questions about the interplay of "emotional proximity and distance" in the Theater of Dionysus, 46. On the character of Electra in the play, see Blundell 1989, 179–80.

36. See Blundell 1989, 12: "Such [moral] conflict can only be resolved by persuasion, which may induce one of the participants to alter or even abandon a decision or moral principle. . . . These speeches rarely succeed, usually because of the intransigence of one or more central characters. Such doomed attempts at persuasion are a characteristically Sophoclean means of effecting tragic pathos and suspense, and at the same time provide a forum for the revelation of moral character and the airing of ethical issues."

37. Woodard 1964, 166.

38. Segal 1966, 479, says of this scene (634–763): "not only the vital hinge of the plot, but, with its complex reversals of life and death, appearance and reality, is also a microcosm of the action of the rest of the play." See also Seale 1982, 65.

39. See Segal 1981, 268–69.

40. Finglass 2007, 341.

41. See Gellie 1972, 116–17 on the *logos/ergon* polarity in the speech.

42. For the metatheatrical elements in this scene, see Ringer 1999, 163–72.

43. On the reflection of Athenian society through its metatheatrical gestures in its dramas, see Falkner 1998, especially 55.

44. Burton 1980, 206; on the structure of the chorus, see also Finglass 2007, 356–57.

45. On the use of mythical exempla here, see Finglass 2007, 360–61.

46. Finglass 2007, 370–73, 437–38, has a thorough discussion of the repetitions in this section.

47. Burton 1980, 214; Segal 1981, 278–80; Seale 1982, 69–70.

48. For the polarity *logos/ergon* in the urn scene and more generally in the play, see Segal 1981, 283–89.

49. See Kitzinger 1991, 300–2, 322–23. Her persuasive reading sees the Paedagogus's lie as "a pivotal moment in the play's structure [that] reveals a way of understanding each of the other scenes" (301). About the effect of the urn scene on our perception of Electra, she notes, "There could be no more effective way for Sophokles to undermine Electra's power, to make it peripheral to the action instead of its center" (323).

50. For the metatheatrical elements in the scene with the urn, see Scodel 1984, 81–82.

51. Finglass 2007, 470–71.

52. On this anomaly, see Goldhill 2012, 98–100.

53. See Foley 2001, 166–68, on the seductive power of Electra's lamentation and its effect on Orestes.

54. Gellie 1972, 125–27, has an insightful discussion of Electra's character in this scene.

55. See n. 61, below.

56. On the downplaying of the matricide, see Gellie 1972, 119–21; Lloyd 2005, 101–2.

57. Finglass 2007, 510–12.

58. A similar substitution occurs in *Philoctetes* at line 51. See below, p. 46.

59. Finglass 2007, 546.

60. E.g., Gellie 1972, 127.

61. There is no clear consensus about the tone of the ending. See Kitzinger 1991, 298–99 and Lloyd 2005, 99–115 for a good summary of the range of opinions. March 2001, 15–20, argues for a positive tone, with references. On Electra's desire for revenge, see the excellent discussion in Lloyd 2005, 92–96. See also Kitto 1950, 128–32; Burton 1980, 220; Woodard 1964, 214–17; Segal 1981, 249–50; Seale 1982, 77–78; Blundell 1989, 178–83. Winnington-Ingram 1980, 225–28, emphasizes allusions to Aeschylus as the basis for a much darker view. For a more balanced perspective, see Finglass 2007, 8–10. Goldhill 2012, 18–21, analyzes the ending, particularly its implications for the character of Electra, as an example of Sophocles's ironic use of *lusis*, "release," in in his plays. See also Goldhill 2012, 201–30, a discussion of how nineteenth century productions of *Electra* treated the ending of the play. Griffiths 2012, 79–81, explores the possibility that the treatment of matricide reflects an implicit political commentary on the act as tyranny.

62. See Blundell 1989, 179: "In particular, we must [be] aware of assuming that Sophocles is somehow 'answering' either Aeschylus or Euripides." See further Gellie 1972, 106, 129–30; Kitzinger 1991, 327; Dunn 2012, 101. For a reading that sees Sophocles's play primarily in relation to Aeschylus and Euripides, see Bowra 1944, 212–60.

63. For the "theatrical joke" in the scene, see Gellie 1972, 212.

64. On this duality of genre in the play, see Gellie 1972, 122

65. See Gellie 115–16 on male action and Electra's "sensibilities."

66. See Ringer's thoughtful discussion (1998, 124–25), where he suggests that meta-theatrical elements in *Philoctetes* signal Sophocles's questioning of "the tragic theater's ability to give new life to old myths."

Chapter 3

1. Stanford 1968, 103–17. See also Knox 1964, 124–25; Roisman 2005, 59–61.

2. For the importance of the setting as a reflection of Philoctetes's character, see Jones 1962, 221–22; Seale 1982, 26–27.

3. See further Segal 1981, 295–300; Rose 1992, 282–88; Rehm 2002, 139. Rose's

analysis of the play's opening as a reflection of sophistic anthropological ideas about the nature of civilization is thoughtful and challenging, an effective answer to those critics who have seen any references by Sophocles to contemporary politics as detracting from the play's success as tragedy.

4. Seale 1982, 32.

5. See Rehm 2002, 146; Levine 2003. For parallels to Euripides's *Cyclops*, see Segal 1981, 300–1.

6. For Philoctetes as savage, see Segal 1981, 333–34. "For Philoctetes, however, resistance to persuasion is vital to integrity of spirit. His stubborn refusal of persuasion is an aspect of his savagery, a sub-human quality" (334). On the visual impact of Philoctetes's savage appearance, see Seale 1982, 32.

7. For the contrast, see Segal 1981, 291.

8. On civilization and savagery in the play, see Segal 1981, 303–5.

9. Lines 68–69 specify only that without the bow, Troy cannot be taken. Later, it will emerge that Philoctetes himself must also go to Troy. For the ambiguity, see note 49 below.

10. For Odysseus's character as sophistic, see Blundell 1987; Rose 1992, 305–10; Roisman 2009, 73–74. On possible reflections of Athenian ideals of *paideia* in the struggle for Neoptolemus's allegiance, see Ferrario 2012, 458–60. On the appearance of sophistic ideas in Sophocles in general, see Rose 1992, 279–82; Roisman 2005, 61–67. See also Rose 1976, 83. For a thoughtful assessment of Odysseus's character in the play, see Beye 1970, 68. On the ethical implications of the exchange between Odysseus and Neoptolemus, see Blundell 1989, 184–93.

11. For Odysseus's perversion of the word *gennaios*, see Knox 1964, 125–26.

12. On the Homeric antecedents and their significance, see Knox 1964, 122.

13. For the polarity throughout the play, see Segal 1981, 333–40.

14. For the significance of the polarity in fifth-century Athenian discourse, see Goldhill 1986, 239–42; Wilson 2012.

15. Rose 1992, 311–12, notes that "the use of stories about offspring of famous heroes seems a particular feature of sophistic teaching." On the two Homeric heroes as models for contrasting values, see Knox 1964, 120–22. For Sophocles's inclusion of Neoptolemus as the second conspirator, see Kyriakou 2012, 150–51.

16. See Guthrie 1971, 250–60; Goldhill 1986, 238–40; Rose 1992, 311.

17. On the negative associations of *kerdos*, see Blundell 1989, 187, n. 13.

18. For the connections between the prologue and parodos, see Burton 1980, 228.

19. For a discussion of the antecedents for the story of Philoctetes, see Bowra 1944, 261–63; Whitman 1951, 174–75.

20. On the chorus' duplicitous behavior, see Ringer 1998, 111–12. Kitto 1950 sees the use of the chorus as part of the conspiracy as what makes *Philoctetes* a "masterpiece of the later Greek stage" (305).

21. Burton 1980, 229.

22. Note that Philoctetes suffers from *odunais*, "body pain," (185) the word used of the Cyclops's pain from his wounded eye (*Od.* 9. 415).

23. For the effect of this kind of entrance, see Taplin 1977, 297.

24. See Seale 1982, 29.

25. On this scene see Winnington-Ingram 1980, 297.

26. Segal 1981, 301–3, analyzes the rehabilitation of Philoctetes in Neoptolemus's eyes through the imagery of hunting.

27. On the parallels, see Reinhardt 1979, 168–73; Whitman 1951, 172–73; Ringer 1998, 102–3.

28. On the possible symbolic meaning of Philoctetes's wound, see Wilson 1978, 235–42; Beye 1970, 66–67; Segal 1981, 316–18; Rose 1992, 298, n.55, with bibliography.

29. See Segal 1981, 289–99.

30. Carson 1990, 153–58.

31. On Lemnos and its significance for Philoctetes, see Segal 1981, 311–14, 323; Kyriakou 2012, 150–51.

32. Ringer 1998, 109, compares Neoptolemus's description of the treachery of the Greek leaders to the Paedagogus's narration of the chariot race in *Electra*.

33. Burton 1980, 232.

34. On this exchange, see Rose 1992, 292–93.

35. Ringer 1998, 112–15, has an excellent analysis of this scene. I cannot, however, agree with him that we are to assume that Philoctetes does not hear the fake Merchant's words at 572–79. The deception works better if Philoctetes "overhears" what the Merchant says.

36. See Rehm 2002, 149–50.

37. On the significance of the bow, see Harsh 1960; Segal 1981, 318–22; Ringer 1998, 117–18.

38. So Knox 1964, 130, "The closing words of the stasimon are sung as the two men come out of the cave, and the chorus quickly puts its mask back on . . ." See further Seale 1982, 37; Ringer 1998, 115–16.

39. See Knox 1964, 130–32; Seale 1982, 37–40.

40. For the bow as symbol of friendship, see Rose 1992, 294.

41. On Philoctetes and Herakles, see Reinhardt 1979, 177–78; Segal 1981, 292–95; Kyriakou 2012, 158–64.

42. For the significance of Neoptolemus's use of hexameters, see Bowra 1944, 281; Gellie 1972, 149; Rose 1992, 297, n.54; Ringer 1998, 116–17.

43. For the impact of Philoctetes's fainting, see Rose 1992, 296–97. See Taplin 1978, 112, for a discussion of the "tableau" formed on stage when Philoctetes faints and its visual impact on our understanding of Neoptolemus's character.

44. For death and rebirth in the myths of Lemnos, see Segal 1981, 313–14.

45. So Ringer 1998, 118: "Touching Philoctetes for the first time seems to draw Neoptolemus completely away from the deceptive role he has been playing." See further Rehm 2002, 153 n.190.

46. For the hero's body in Sophocles, see Rehm 2002, 169–70; Van Nortwick 2012, 145–47.

47. Segal 1995, 106. I cannot agree with Woodard 1964, 174, who associates Orestes exclusively with *ergon* and Electra with *logos*. See Kitzinger 1991, 302, n.13.

48. See above, chapter 1, n. 6.

49. On the problems arising from the ambiguity, see Kitto 1956, 95–99; Knox 1964, 126–27, 187–90.

50. It is not clear how this attempt at suicide would be staged. Webster 1970, 130, says that the *ekkyklema* is raised up sufficiently from the level of the area in front of the *skene*, and that this height, plus the fact that the stage was raised higher than the *orchestra* (an assumption that is controversial for the fifth century), would allow the audience to imagine that Philoctetes, standing on the *ekkyklema,* could leap to his death. See also Seale 1982, 27–28.

51. See Rose 1992, 286–88.

52. See Knox 1964, 117; Segal 1981, 296.

53. Beye 1970 offers an intelligent appraisal of the reworking of the Iliadic material in the play. See Blundell 1989, 199–200, for Philoctetes as an "Achilles figure."

54. Burton 1980, 244.

55. Note that Herakles uses the word *muthos*, not *logos*, in describing the message he delivers (1410, 1417), and Philoctetes echoes this gesture at 1447.

56. On the visual impact of Herakles's appearance on the *machina*, see Seale 1982, 45.

57. Ringer 1998, 121–24, discusses the issues raised by Sophocles's use of the deus ex machina here. See also Seale 1982, 46. Roisman 2005, 108–9, suggests that Herakles functions as surrogate father for the lonely hero, a convincing idea, given the prominence of father-son relationships in the play. She also argues (109–11), following Lattimore 1964 (92, n.35), that Herakles is played for the actors on stage by a disguised Odysseus. Though an intriguing suggestion, this interpretation ultimately, as Roisman notes, "gives Odysseus the last word and implies that the play endorses the ethos of deception for the sake of victory" (111), an outcome rather too cynical and bleak, in my view.

58. See Bowra 1944, 301, for the differences between Sophocles's use of the deus ex machina here and its role on Euripides's plays.

59. For Herakles as a "major site of ideological struggle," see Rose 1992, 281, n.25.

60. Compare Athena's visitation to Achilles in *Iliad* 1, where her intervention on behalf of Hera to convince him not to kill Agamemnon preserves Achilles's implacable anger in a way that a change of mind would not. Whitman 1951 says of Philoctetes's eventual acquiescence in the plan to return him to Troy: "The triumph of Philoctetes is that he finds a way to return to the world, without compromising his heroic integrity" (179). I would say rather that *Sophocles* finds a way to preserve Philoctetes's heroic integrity, by bringing Herakles on stage as a representative of transcendent divine will. So Kitto, 1956: "Philoctetes' refusal to go to Troy is dissolved in such a way that his reasons for not going remain valid" (137). On the function of Herakles as deus ex machina, see further Blundell 1989, 223–25.

61. See Segal's suggestive remarks (1981, 331) on the "new" model for heroism embodied by Philoctetes and culminating in the Oedipus of Sophocles's last play.

Chapter 4

1. Some of the ideas in this chapter have appeared earlier in Van Nortwick 2012.

2. So Knox 1964: "His opening speech shows a man who seems to be at the end rather than the beginning" (148).

3. See Knox's characteristically pithy assessment (1964, 144–46).

4. Ringer 1998, 95, describes the play as an "antitragedy." See also Hesk 2012, 173.

5. E.g., Taplin 1977; Seale 1982; Ringer 1998; Wiles 1997; Rehm 2002.

6. Wiles 1997, 146–53.

7. On the importance of setting in the beginning of the play, see Kitto 1950, 401; Jones 1962, 218–20; Vidal-Naquet 1988, 354–59; Dunn 1992, 1–8; Kelly 2009, 122–23; Hesk 2012, 174–77.

8. Wiles 1997, 147, n.53.

9. See Vidal-Naquet 1988, 334–39; Zeitlin 1990, 144–50.

10. On *deinos*, see Guthrie 1971, 32.

11. *Il. 11. 654; Eur. Med. 44.* See above, chapter 1, p. 4.

12. Edmunds 1996, 43; Burton 1980, 258. The figure of the old man walking across the stage to deliver important, often devastating news, connects all three of Sophocles's Theban plays, from Tiresias in *Antigone*, to the same character in *Oedipus Tyrannus*, followed by the Corinthian and Theban messengers in the same play, and finally to Creon and Oedipus himself in *Oedipus at Colonus*.

13. For a discussion of Oedipus's self-defense and its relationship to issues raised in *Oedipus Tyrannus*, see Jones 1962, 229–33; Kelly 2009, 45–49.

14. For the meaning of *hieros*, see Burkert 1985, 269.

15. For parallels between Oedipus and Philoctetes, see Jones 1962, 218. On Oedipus's fear of being marginalized as "other," see Van Nortwick 1989, 134–35, 139, 152.

16. See Jones 1962: "The action is therefore poised on the brink of fulfillment by Oedipus's arrival at Colonus in the opening lines" (222–23).

17. Knox 1964 sees a transformation in Oedipus over the course of the play, through which he assumes while alive the powers of a *heros*, "a superhuman being, a spirit which lives on with the power over the affairs of men after the death of the body" (147); so also, Bowra 1944, 307–8, 354. This model is a good way to fit the character into existing Greek religious beliefs but leads, in my view, to an incomplete picture of Sophocles's innovation. Knox's version of the old hero tends to stress the irascible part of Oedipus's temperament, his "heroic temper," which then modulates into a semi-divine anger ("a daemonic, superhuman wrath" 159), while underestimating the striking originality of Sophocles's vision of Oedipus's position as a mortal in relationship to other forces in the universe. Likewise, Bowra 1944 sees the entire play as the "heroization" of Oedipus, leading him to understand the old hero as some kind of supernatural being even before

his death, e.g., "Foreknowledge of the future belongs to Oedipus because he is already more than a man" (338). I would insist that we must understand Oedipus's character and perspective as striking but entirely consistent with human experience. See also Knox's discussion of other scholarship at 193–94, n.11 and, more recently, Kelly 2009, 41–45; 79–85.

18. Burton 1980, 261.

19. Knox 1964, 152; Blundell 1989, 248–49. Scholars have argued over whether Theseus actually offers Oedipus citizenship or only protection, with much of the discussion centered on whether line 637 has *empolin*, "citizen," or *empalin*, "on the contrary." See Burian 1974; Vidal-Naquet 1988, 339–54; Wilson 1997, 63–90; Kelly 2009, 78, n.49.

20. For *Oedipus at Colonus* as a suppliant play, see Burian 1974; Wilson 1997; Kelly 2009, 75–79; Hesk 2012, 179–81.

21. For Oedipus as "the master of time" in this speech see Zeitlin 1990, 163–67.

22. Burton 1980, 275.

23. See Knox 1964, 155–56, an eloquent appraisal of the ode.

24. For a thorough discussion of Creon's behavior, see Blundell 1989, 234–38. See also Kelly's insightful remarks (2009, 116–18).

25. So Bowra 1944, 331–32.

26. *Deinos* was used to describe the clever, sophistic speaker. See Guthrie 1971, 32–33.

27. On Creon and the Odysseus of *Philoctetes*, see Blundell 1989, 233–34.

28. See Whitman 1951, 196–97. On Theseus as model king, see Kelly 2009, 110–16.

29. Burton 1980, 281.

30. See Rehm 1992, 61 on the role of imagination in choral lyrics.

31. See Zeitlin 1990, 160–61 for Polyneices's approach to his father.

32. I cannot agree with Knox 1964, 120: ". . . in *Oedipus at Colonus* it would have made little difference to our feelings if the order [of the Creon and Polyneices episodes] had been reversed—if Polyneices had tried to use force and Creon had limited his attempt to persuasion and deceit." The order of the supplications is in this case crucial to the meaning of Oedipus's life and death.

33. See Falkner 1995, esp. 211–59.

34. See Blundell 1989, 241; Burian 1974, 422–23.

35. E.g., Adams 1957, 173–74; Whitman 1951, 211–12. Easterling 1967 sees Polyneices as at fault but also understands Sophocles to be eliciting our sympathy for his being cursed. Blundell 1989 finds Sophocles's portrayal of Polyneices's case "ambivalent" (243–45), as does Kelly 2009, 118–21. Hesk 2012, 181–85, has a thoughtful discussion of Oedipus's reaction to Polyneices.

36. See Van Nortwick 1989, 141, n. 17.

37. See further Van Nortwick 2008, 144–57.

38. For the resemblance of Polyneices to Oedipus, see Winnington-Ingram 1980, 277; Blundell 1989, 247–48; Kelly 2009, 121.

39. Scott 1996, 239, suggests that the final stanza of the choral ode (1211–48) has

been interrupted by the arrival of Polyneices, further marking off the scene as an unexpected intrusion.

40. Reinhardt 1979, 200–2; Segal 1981, 389; Zeitlin 1990, 162; Ringer 1998, 97.

41. See Ringer 1998, 94–95, for other kinds of metatheatrical gesture in the play.

42. See further Scott 1996, 240–44.

43. On Oedipus's last moments, see further Zeitlin 1990, 155–67.

44. One is reminded of the end of the *Iliad*, where the meeting of Achilles and Priam creates a sense of aesthetic closure, but always in the shadow of the war coming twelve days hence. See also Burton 1980, 270.

45. E.g., Jebb 1900, xliii. Kitto 1950, 386–87, grants the episodic nature of the play but denies that it lacks unity, saying that "no play shows more strength." See also his insightful remarks on form and meaning (1956, 87–91). For a positive view of the play's structure, see Kelly 2009, 85.

46. See Gellie 1972, 112.

47. Zeitlin 1990, 157, compares Oedipus's escape from endless repetition of the past to the solution offered by the law courts in Aeschylus's *Eumenides*. Segal 1981 has argued the Oedipus of the last play symbolizes the entire genre of tragedy: "By returning to this figure whose life contains the most extreme of tragic reversals, Sophocles seems to be consciously reflecting upon and transcending the tragic pattern which he did so much to develop (406)." See also Whitman 1951, 191.

48. Hyde 1980, 14.

49. Ibid. 37.

50. See further Ringer 1998, 91: "[Sophocles's] use of Colonus represents an example of an ancient dramatist 'staging' his home and polis, endeavoring to preserve it, through dramatic action and poetry, from the ravages of war and time." Sophocles too is creating a gift circle. See further Van Nortwick 1998, 152.

51. Whitman 1951 resists the idea that Sophocles projects the hero's fate as finally mysterious. Rather, he insists that these heroes, and especially the aged Oedipus, are heroic because of their inner worth, however painfully tested. See especially 213–14.

Chapter 5

1. Thuc. 5. 84–116; 6–7.

2. See Ferrario 2012, 450–58, for a balanced survey of the evidence and scholarship. For *Philoctetes* and the oligarchic revolution, see Ringer 1998, 102–3; Rehm 2002, 154–55; Rose 1992, 327–30; Roisman 2005, 67–69. Kelly 2009, 14–18, has a good summary of the possible historical connections between *Oedipus at Colonus* and events in Athens. Vickers 2008 makes the strongest claims for topicality, but his attempt to find specific references to Alcibiades in the plays is not convincing to me.

3. See Rehm 1992, 73–74.

4. See Finley 1938, 55–60; Goldhill 1986, 240–41.

5. See Ferrario 2012, 460–61

6. See Foley's thoughtful remarks (2001, 170–71) on the possible political connotations of Electra's lament in Athens.

7. See Seale 1982, 50, on the prominent representation of suffering in *Philoctetes*, which is focused on the hero's body.

8. Edmunds 1996, 41.

9. See the challenging discussion of the idea of "late work" in McMullan 2007, especially 1–64, with extensive bibliography.

10. See further Landon 1999.

11. Said 2006, 7.

12. E.g., McMullan 2007, 1–4.

13. See Said 2006, 7–8; Solomon 2003, 3–5. For Sophocles and Beethoven, see also the suggestive remarks of Kitto 1950, 390–91.

14. Knox 1964, 1–57. See also 177, of Philoctetes: "The tragic hero hews to the pattern; but the situation in which he is placed is unique." I agree for the most part with this distinction between the *temperament* of the Sophoclean hero and the *context* within which s/he exerts him/herself.

References

Adams, S. 1957. *Sophocles the Playwright*. Toronto: University of Toronto Press.

Beer, J. 2004. *Sophocles and the Tragedy of Athenian Democracy*. Westport and London: Praeger.

Beye, C. 1970. "Sophocles' *Philoctetes* and the Homeric Embassy." *Transactions and Proceedings of the American Philological Association* 101, 63–76.

Blundell, M. 1987. "The moral character of Odysseus in *Philoctetes.*" *Greek, Roman, and Byzantine Studies* 28, 307–29.

Blundell, M. 1989. *Helping Friends and Harming Enemies: A Study in Sophocles and Greek Ethics*. Cambridge: Cambridge University Press.

Bowra, C. 1944. *Sophoclean Tragedy*. Oxford: Oxford University Press.

Burian, P. 1974. "Suppliant and savior." *Phoenix* 28, 408–29.

Burkert, W. 1985. *Greek Religion*. Trans. J. Raffan. Cambridge, MA: Harvard University Press.

Burton, R.W.B. 1980. *The Chorus in Sophocles' Tragedies*. Oxford: Oxford University Press.

Carson, A. 1990. "Putting Her in Her Place: Woman, Dirt, and Desire." In *Before Sexuality: The Construction of Erotic Experience in the Ancient Greek World*, ed. D. Halperin, J. Winkler, and F. Zeitlin. Princeton: Princeton University Press, 135–69.

Dale, A. 1968. *The Lyric Meters of Greek Drama*, 2nd ed. Cambridge: Cambridge University Press.

Dale, A. 1971 and 1981. "Metrical Analysis of Tragic Choruses." *Bulletin of the Institute for Classical Studies*. Supplement 21.1 and 2.

Dunn, F. 1992. "Introduction: Beginning at Colonus." *Yale Classical Studies* 29, 1–12.

Dunn, F. 2012. "Electra." In *A Companion to Sophocles*, ed. K. Ormand. West Sussex: Wiley-Blackwell, 98–110.

Easterling, P. 1967. "Oedipus and Polyneices." *Proceedings of the Cambridge Philological Society* 193, 1–13.

Edmunds, L. 1996. *Theatrical Space and Historical Space in Sophocles'* Oedipus at Colonus. Lanham, MD: Rowman & Littlefield.

Falkner, T. 1995. *The Poetics of Old Age in Greek Epic, Lyric, and Tragedy*. Norman and London: University of Oklahoma Press.

Falkner, T. 1998. "Containing Tragedy: Rhetoric and Self-Representation in Sophocles' *Philoctetes*." *Classical Antiquity* 17, 25–58.

Ferrario, S. 2012. "Political Tragedy: Sophocles and Athenian History." In *Brill's Companion to Sophocles*, ed. A. Markantonatos. Leiden and Boston: Brill, 447–70.

Finglass, P. 2007. *Sophocles: Electra*. Cambridge: Cambridge University Press.

Finglass, P. 2011. *Sophocles: Ajax*. Cambridge: Cambridge University Press.

Finley, J. 1938. "Euripides and Thucydides." *Harvard Studies in Classical Philology* 49, 23–68.

Finley, J. 1939. "The Origins of Thucydides' Style." *Harvard Studies in Classical Philology* 50, 35–84.

Foley, H. 2001. *Female Acts in Greek Tragedy*. Princeton: Princeton University Press.

Gamel, M. 2002. "From the *Thesomphorizusai* to the *Julie Thesmo Show*: Adaptation, Performance, Reception." *American Journal of Philology* 123. 2, 465–99.

Gellie, G. 1972. *Sophocles: A Reading*. Melbourne: Melbourne University Press.

Goldhill, S. 1986. *Reading Greek Tragedy*. Cambridge: Cambridge University Press.

Goldhill, S. 2012. *Sophocles and the Language of Tragedy*. Oxford: Oxford University Press.

Griffiths, E. 2012. "*Electra*." In *Brill's Companion to Sophocles*, ed. A. Markanonatos. Leiden and Boston: Brill, 72–91.

Guthrie, W. 1971. *The Sophists*. Cambridge: Cambridge University Press.

Hall, E. 2006. *The Theatrical Cast of Athens: Interactions between Ancient Greek Drama and Society*. Oxford: Oxford University Press.

Harsh, P. 1960. "The Role of the Bow in the *Philoctetes* of Sophocles." *American Journal of Philology* 81, 408–14.

Hesk, J. 2012. "*Oedipus at Colonus*." In *Brill's Companion to Sophocles*, ed. A. Markanonatos. Leiden and Boston: Brill, 167–89.

Hutchinson, G. O. 1999. "Sophocles and Time." In *Sophocles Revisited*, ed. J. Griffin. Oxford: Oxford University Press, 47–72.

Hyde, L. 1980. *The Gift*. New York: Random House.

Inoue, I. 2009. "The Players Will Tell All: The Dramatist, the Actors and the Art of Acting in Sophocles' *Philoctetes*." In *Sophocles and the Greek Tragic Tradition*, ed. S. Goldhill and E. Hall. Cambridge: Cambridge University Press, 48–68.

Jacobsen, T. 1976. *The Treasures of Darkness*. New Haven: Yale University Press.

Jebb, R. 1900. *Sophocles: The Plays and Fragments, Part II: The Oedipus at Colonus*. Cambridge: Cambridge University Press.

Jones, J. 1962. *On Aristotle and Greek Tragedy*. Oxford: Oxford University Press.

Kelly, A. 2009. *Sophocles: Oedipus at Colonus*. London: Duckworth.

Kirkwood, G. 1958. *A Study in Sophoclean Drama*. Ithaca: Cornell University Press.

Kitto, H. 1950. *Greek Tragedy*. London: Methuen.

Kitto, H. 1956. *Form and Meaning in Drama*. London: Methuen.

Kitzinger, M. 1991. "Why Mourning Becomes Electra." *California Studies in Classical Philology* 10.2, 298–327.

Kitzinger, M. 2008. *The Choruses of Sophokles'* Antigone *and* Philoktetes. Leiden: Brill.

Knox, B. 1964. *The Heroic Temper: Studies in Sophoclean Tragedy*. Berkeley and Los Angeles: University of California Press.

Kyriakou, P. 2012. "*Philoctetes*." In *Brill's Companion to Sophocles*, ed. A. Markanonatos. Leiden and Boston: Brill, 149–66.

Landon, H. 1999. *Mozart's Last Year*. New York: Thames & Hudson.

Lattimore, R. 1964. *Story Patterns in Greek Tragedy*. London: Athlone Press.

Levine, D. 2003. "Sophocles' *Philoctetes* and *Odyssey* 9: Odysseus vs. the Cave Man." *Scholia* 12, 3–26.

Lloyd, M. 2005. *Sophocles:* Electra. London: Duckworth.

March, J. 2001. *Sophocles:* Electra. Warminster: Aris and Phillips.

McMullan, G. 2007. *Shakespeare and the Idea of Late Writing*. Cambridge: Cambridge University Press.

Ormand, K. 1999. *Exchange and the Maiden: Marriage in Sophoclean Tragedy*. Austin: University of Texas Press.

Padel, R. 1990. "Making Space Speak." In *Nothing to Do with Dionysos? Athenian Drama in Its Social Context*, ed. J. Winkler and F. Zeitlin. Princeton: Princeton University Press.

Parry, A. 1981. Logos *and* Ergon *in Thucydides*. New York: Arno Press.

Race, W. 1981. "The Word Καιρός in Greek Drama." *Transactions and Proceedings of the American Philological Association* 111, 197–214.

Rehm, R. 1992. *Greek Tragic Theater*. London: Routledge.

Rehm, R. 2002. *The Play of Space*. Princeton: Princeton University Press.

Reinhardt, K. 1979. *Sophocles*. Trans. Hazel and David Harvey. New York: Barnes & Noble.

Ringer, M. 1998. *Electra and the Empty Urn: Metatheater and Role Playing in Sophocles*. Chapel Hill and London: University of North Carolina Press.

Roisman, H. 2005. *Sophocles: Philoctetes*. London: Duckworth.

Rose, P. 1976. "Sophocles' *Philoctetes* and the Teachings of the Sophists." *Harvard Studies in Classical Philology* 80, 48–105.

Rose, P. 1992. *Sons of the Gods, Children of the Earth: Ideology and Literary Form in Ancient Greece*. Ithaca: Cornell University Press.

Said, E. 2006. *On Late Style*. New York: Random House.

Schein, S. 2012. "Sophocles and Homer." In *A Companion to Sophocles*, ed. K. Ormand. West Sussex: Wiley-Blackwell, 424–39.

Scodel, R. 1984. *Sophocles*. Boston: Twayne Publishers.

Scodel, R . 2012. "Sophocles' Biography." In *A Companion to Sophocles*, ed. K. Ormand. West Sussex: Wiley-Blackwell, 25–37.

Scott, W. 1996. *Musical Design in Sophoclean Theater*. Hanover and London: University Press of New England.

Seaford, R. 1985. "The Destruction of Limits in Sophokles' *Elektra*." *Classical Quarterly* 35, 315–23.

Seale, D. 1982. *Vision and Stagecraft in Sophocles*. Chicago: University of Chicago Press.

Segal, C. 1966. "The *Electra* of Sophocles." *Transactions and Proceedings of the American Philological Association* 97, 473–545.

Segal, C. 1981. *Tragedy and Civilization: An Interpretation of Sophocles*. Cambridge, MA: Harvard University Press.

Segal, C. 1995. "Philoctetes and the Imperishable Piety." In *Sophocles' Tragic World*. Cambridge, MA: Harvard University Press, 95–119.

Solomon, M. 2003. *Late Beethoven*. Berkeley: University of California Press.

Stanford, W. 1968. *The Ulysses Theme*. Ann Arbor: University of Michigan Press.

Taplin, O. 1977. *Stagecraft in Aeschylus*. Oxford: Oxford University Press.

Taplin, O. 1978. *Greek Tragedy in Action*. Berkeley: University of California Press.

Van Nortwick, T. 1989. "Do Not Go Gently: *Oedipus at Colonus* and the Psychology of Aging." In *Old Age in Greek and Latin Literature*, ed. T. Falkner and J. de Luce. Albany: State University of New York Press, 132–56.

Van Nortwick, T. 1992. *Somewhere I Have Never Travelled: The Second Self and the Hero's Journey in Ancient Epic*. New York: Oxford University Press.

Van Nortwick, T. 1998. *Oedipus: The Meaning of a Masculine Life*. Norman and London: University of Oklahoma Press.

Van Nortwick, T. 2008. *Imagining Men: Ideals of Masculinity in Ancient Greek Culture*. Westport: Praeger Press.

Van Nortwick, T. 2009. *The Unknown Odysseus: Alternate Worlds in Homer's Odyssey*. Ann Arbor: University of Michigan Press.

Van Nortwick, T. 2012. "Last Things: *Oedipus at Colonus* and the End of Tragedy." In *A Companion to Sophocles*, ed. K. Ormand. West Sussex: Wiley-Blackwell, 141–54.

Vickers, M. 2008. *Sophocles and Alcibiades: Athenian Politics in Ancient Greek Literature*. Ithaca: Cornell University Press.

Vidal-Naquet, P. 1988. "Oedipus between Two Cities: An Essay on *Oedipus at Colonus*." In *Myth and Tragedy in Ancient Greece*, ed. J. Vernant and P. Vidal-Naquet. Trans. J. Lloyd. New York: Zone Books.

Webster, T. 1970. *Sophocles: Philoctetes*. Cambridge: Cambridge University Press.

Wiles, D. 1997. *Tragedy in Athens*. Cambridge: Cambridge University Press.

Whitman, C. 1951. *Sophocles: A Study of Heroic Humanism*. Cambridge, MA: Harvard University Press.

Wilson, E. 2012. "Sophocles and Philosophy." In *Brill's Companion to Sophocles*, ed. A. Markantonatos. Leiden and Boston: Brill, 537–62.

Wilson, E. 1978. *The Wound and the Bow.* New York: Farrar, Straus and Giroux.

Wilson, J. 1997. *The Hero and the City: An Interpretation of Sophocles'* Oedipus at Colonus. Ann Arbor: University of Michigan Press.

Winngton-Ingram, R. 1980. *Sophocles: An Interpretation.* Cambridge: Cambridge University Press.

Woodard, T. 1964. "*Electra* by Sophocles: The Dialectical Design." *Harvard Studies in Classical Philology* 68, 163–205.

Woodard, T. 1965. "*Electra* by Sophocles: The Dialectical Design (Part II)." *Harvard Studies in Classical Philology* 70, 195–233.

Zeitlin, F. 1990. "Thebes: Theater of Self and Society in Athenian Drama." In *Nothing to Do with Dionysos? Athenian Drama in Its Social Context*, ed. J. Winkler and F. Zeitlin. Princeton: Princeton University Press, 130–67.

Index

Acropolis, 81

Aegisthus: as usurper, 14; murder of, 34–35

Aeschylus: *Agamemnon*, 14; characterization in the plays of, 20; *Eumenides*, 78; *Libation Bearers*, 12; *Oresteia*, 13

Achilles, 9, 40, 48, 54, 66, 86, 90, 117

Agamemnon, 11, 18, 19, 55, 117

Ajax, 48, 53, 96, 117

Alcmaeon, 26

Amphiarius, 26

Andromache, 13

Antigone: captured by Creon, 98; guide for Oedipus, 81, 86–87, 90; lament of, 110; rescued by Theseus, 101; supporter of Polyneices, 102

antilabē, 26, 30

Antilochus, 53

Apollo, 8, 22, 36, 57, 79, 85, 101

aretē, 47, 58

Arginusae, 115

Argos, 101, 105

Aristophanes: *Lysistrata*, 116

Artemis, 36

artist in old age, 120

Athenian democracy: challenging traditional beliefs, 9; reflected in Athenian tragic drama, viii, 25, 41, 64, 117

Athens, 84, 88, 89, 95, 100, 115, 118

Beethoven, 121

Calypso, 17

characterization: of Clytemnestra, 20–21; of Electra, ix, 20–21, 31–33, 35–36, 38; of Oedipus, 92–93, 102, 109; of Philoctetes, 44–45, 48–52, 71–73, 76, 78

chorus: in *Antigone*, 11; and characterization, ix; coda of as suspect, 35; entrance of in *Electra*, 11; entrance of in *Oedipus at Colonus*, 85; entrance of in *Philoctetes*, 48; formal elements, ix, 11; make-up of in *Philoctetes*, 48; part of deception in *Philoctetes*, 51, 53, 55, 59, 62; scholarship about, 125 n. 5; supporters of Electra, 11; *Women of Trachis*, 12

chronos, 17, 21, 28

Chrysothemis: and Electra, 15–17, 26; modelled on Antigone, 15

Circe, 17

Clytemnestra: in Aeschylus's *Oresteia*, 13; antecedent for Electra, 2; and Electra, 18–22; murder of, 34; masculine traits of, 116; murderer, 11, 18; and Orestes, 24; self-defense of, 19–20

Colonus, 84, 97

comic narrative: ironic detachment in, 39; restoration of order in, 39

Creon, 91, 92, 97–99, 117

daemon, 105

deceit: in comic narrative, 39; language of, 47; tool of hero's enemies, 23, 29, 31, 47, 53, 56, 62, 74, 119

Decelea, 115

145

Deianira: antecedent for Electra, 2; faithful wife, 13

deinos, 86

Demeter, 109

deus ex machina: in Euripides, 77–78; Herakles as, 77–78, 122; in Sophocles, 77, 122

Diomedes, 53, 56

disguise: in comic narrative, 39–40

Electra: and Antigone, 15; authenticity undermined, 29, 33, 38; and Calypso, 17; champion of traditional heroic values, 16, 29; and the chorus, 11, 14; and Chrysothemis, 15–17; and Circe, 17; and Clytemnestra, 17–22; compared to Achilles, 41; compared to Oedipus, 82, 96–97; compared to Philoctetes, 47, 49, 50–51, 73, 76, 79, 96–97; end to isolation of, 33; entrance of, 10; separated from revenge plot, 38; similar to Clytemnestra, 24–25; and time, 10, 17; tragic hero, 12–14, 21–22, 38, 40–41; virgin, 13; woman who waits for a man to return, 13

Epic of Gilgamesh, viii

Erinyes, 10, 37, 105

Eriphyle, 26

Eteocles, 90, 92

Eumenides: grove of, vii, 83, 84, 85, 93, 100, 109, 118

Euripides: *Electra*, 34, 77, 115; *Helen*, 13; *Iphigenia in Aulis*, 116; *Iphigenia in Tauris*, 116; *Medea*, 116; *Orestes*, 78; *Trojan Women*, 116

gender differences: Greek beliefs about, 16–17, 38, 51, 116

gifts: circulation of as bond in *Oedipus at Colonus*, 111–13, 123

gods: in Sophoclean drama, 36, 69; will of, 52, 55, 69, 71–72, 82, 122

Great Lakes Theater Company, ix, xi

Greek epic poetry, viii

Hades, 10, 109

Hector, 64

Helen: bad wife, 13; in Euripides's *Orestes*, 78

Helenus, 56, 68, 76

Hermes, 10, 33, 36

Herakles: agent of divine will, 68, 72, 76–77; body of, 64; bow of, 45, 57, 60; problematic hero, 14

hero: body of as catalyst for new awareness in others, 63–65, 69, 78, 82, 117; place in community, 63–64

Homer
    Iliad, 9, 64
    Odyssey, 12
    as comic narrative, 39
    and first version of Orestes myth, 36

Homeric heroes as models in *Philoctetes*, 54, 66–67

Hyde, Lewis, 112

Ibsen, 121

Iphianassa, 11

Ismene, 90, 91, 98, 101, 111

Ixion, 59

justice: in *Electra*, 20, 25, 27, 36–37, 41

kairos, 8, 17, 21, 28, 31, 48, 61, 96, 109

katabasis, 60–63

kerdos, 16, 24, 26, 27, 35, 47, 48, 92, 97, 106, 112

kleos, 8, 27, 88

Lemnian women, 51

logos: and *ergon*, 9, 15–16, 23, 25, 29, 35, 38, 45–46, 53, 57, 58, 61, 65, 75, 98, 117

Medea, 86, 116

Melians, 115

Menelaus, 56, 78, 117

metatheatrical elements: in *Electra*, 31; in *Oedipus at Colonus*, 107; in *Philoctetes*, 55–56, 68

mortality: human knowledge of, viii; in tragic narrative, 39

Mount Cithaeron, 83

Mozart, 120

myth: as background for plot, 8, 41, 58–59, 78, 104

Neoptolemus: adverse to deceit, 45; agent of *logos*, 117; battle for the soul of, 47, 59–60, 66–67, 71, 118; compared to Orestes, 64–65; compared to Polyneices, 111; heroic, 54; son of Achilles, 45–46, 66

Nestor, 53

Nicias, Peace of, 115
Niobe, 11
nomos: and *phusis*, 47

Odysseus: agent of *logos*, 117; deceitful, 8, 43; disguise of, 40; mentor for Neoptolemus, 45–47, 51; name, 88; and the Paedagogus, 46; sophistic, 46–47, 67, 74, 118
Oedipus: aged hero, 105; anger of, 102, 104–5; body as gift to Athens, 94–95, 97, 110, 118; compared to Electra, 82, 96–97; compared to Philoctetes, 82, 89–90, 96–97, 118; compared to Polyneices, 105; conduit for divine will, 91, 112–13; as *daemon*, 105; death of, 109; grave, 96, 97, 108; last walk, vii, 108–9; liminal, 84–85; past as problematic, 86–89, 92, 94; sacred, 89, 101; self-defense of, 88–89, 92, 94, 100; suppliant, 95, 102; transcendent, 107, 111; untypical hero, 81–82; 92, 113
old age in Greek tragedy, 102
oracles, 8, 67, 68, 91, 94
Orestes: agent of *logos*, 117; ashes of, 29; body of, 64; and Clytemnestra, 24; comic, 40; compared to Hermes, 37; entrance of, 7–9, 11; false recognitions of, 39; and horsemanship, 19, 20, 22–23; not a tragic hero, 12, 16; pulled into Electra's emotions, 31–32; recognition of, 29–30; relationship with Electra, 28–30; return of, 28–33

Paeadagogus, 7, 8, 22, 29, 31, 32, 39, 117
parodos, 11
Patroclus, 64
Penelope: antecedent for Electra, 2; faithful wife, 13; left out of plotting, 31
Persephone, 10, 109
performance: scholarship about, 125 n. 4
Philoctetes: body of, 63–65; bow of, 52, 55, 57–58, 60, 68, 74; civilized, 50; compared to Achilles, 71; compared to Electra, 47, 49, 50–51, 73, 76, 79, 97; compared to Oedipus, 82, 89–90, 96–97, 118; compared to Polyphemus, 43–44, 49–50, 72, 117; entrance of, 49; feminized, 50–51; mentor for Neoptolemus, 50; savage, 49–50, 51, 117; symbolic death of, 61, 65; as warrior, 50; wound, 49, 51, 117

Phoenix, 55, 66
phusis, 23, 46–47, 66, 67
Polyneices, 90, 92, 101–7, 111, 117, 119
Polyphemus, 43–44, 49–50, 72, 117
Poseidon, 84, 99, 102
Priam, 65
Procne, 10
Prometheus, 84
Pylades, 7, 78, 117

recognition scene: dynamics of, 30–31
revenge story: in *Electra*, 7–8, 22–23; moral content of in *Electra* compared to that in Aeschylus's *Oresteia* and Euripides's *Electra* 35–37; motivation in, 25

Said, Edward, 120
Sarpedon, 64
Shakespeare, 121
Sicilian Expedition, 115, 116
skēnē, vii, 7, 8, 43, 84
Sophists, 9, 67, 116
Sophoclean tragic hero: defying larger forces, vii, 76–77, 122; Electra as, 12–14; evolution of, vii, 75–76, 78–79, 80, 84, 90, 121–23; focus of audience perspective, 40; inwardness of, 117; lacking heroic agency, 116; and the meaning of human life, vii, 85, 113, 121; Oedipus as, 80, 81; Philoctetes as, 71–73, 75, 79–80; scholarship about, ix, 125 n. 7; separation from main action of plot, 4–5, 12, 38, 41, 51–52, 58, 76, 82, 118–19; will of balanced by the need for community, viii, 112–13
Sophocles: *Ajax*, 38–39, 48, 63–64, 77, 96; *Antigone*, 11, 64, 105; chronology of plays, 1; death of, 115; depth of characterization in plays of, 21; *Electra*, 7–41, 64–65; innovative use of chorus, 31–32, 48, 87, 93, 99; 108; late work, 121–23; life of, 5, 115; *Oedipus at Colonus*, 81–113; *Oedipus Tyrannus*, 84, 88, 89, 93; *Philoctetes*, 43–80; *Women of Trachis*, 11, 64
Sparta, 115

Teiresias, 97, 116
Theater of Dionysus, vii, 82–83, 89, 115
Thebes, 83, 90, 95, 100, 101
Thersites, 53

Theseus, 55, 83, 91, 95, 96, 97, 99, 102, 108, 110, 111
Thucydides, 115, 116
time: cyclical for hero, 12, 17, 51, 96
tragic drama: as vehicle for reflecting Athenian society, 25, 41, 51, 64, 117
tragic narrative, 39, 122

unburied corpse: in Homer, 63; in Sophocles, 63–65

virtue: can it be taught, 9, 47, 67

Wiles, David, 82

Zeus, 101, 109